A · GUIDE · TO
GRAND CANYON
NATIONAL PARK AND VICINITY

Copyright © 1997 by Grand Canyon Association
Post Office Box 399, Grand Canyon, Arizona 86023
(520) 638-2481
All rights reserved.
First edition

ISBN 0-938216-57-0

Library of Congress Catalog Card Number 97-77767

Produced for Grand Canyon Association by Sandra Scott
 Publishing Services.
Text by Sandra Scott.
Editorial review by Pam Frazier and Greer Price.
Book design by Christina Watkins.
Typography and production by Penny Smith, TypeWorks.
Raven illustration on cover by Lawrence Ormsby.
Lithography by Courier Graphics, Inc., Phoenix, Arizona.

Printed on recycled paper.

All maps in text by the DLF Group. Illustrated map inside
back cover © by Robert W. Tope, Natural Science
Illustrations in collaboration with the DLF Group.

All photographs in text courtesy of National Park Service
unless otherwise noted.

*Thanks to everyone who helped bring it all together, espe-
cially Mike Anderson, Jan Balsom, Carl Bowman, Anita
Davis, and Gary Ladd who reviewed natural and human
history; Jane Gillespie for expediting information from
concessioners; Sara Stebbins for library and research
guidance; Susan Lamb and Christina Watkins for untiring
support; the dozens of NPS and USFS folks who took time
to answer questions; and Greer Price, whose help went far
beyond the call.*   *S.S.*

Grand Canyon

■ CONTENTS

CONTENTS

For up-to-date information on park facilities, services, and programs, check the Grand Canyon National Park website online at www.thecanyon.com/nps

■ INTRODUCTION

Grand Canyon conveys a different message to its every viewer. That is the way of masterpieces. Artists respond to it with paint, pen, and melody; scientists, with questions and answers. American Indians who hold the Canyon sacred believe they cannot approach it without observing cleansing and preparatory ceremonies. The Canyon is so powerful that for them to do otherwise would be dangerous. The Canyon speaks through silence, and its realization isn't an assault on the senses, but a dawning. Comprehension of its vastness takes a little while—flawless proportions mask its immensity; depth is balanced by width. But as you watch, something—a sound, a movement—will bring focus.

The steepness of its topography has created five of North America's seven life zones and three of its four deserts within park boundaries. Here are forests, streams, waterfalls, alpine meadows, deserts, canyons, and plateaus. Numerous overlooks give access to some of the world's most spectacular scenery. There are hundreds of miles of hiking trails and one of the world's longest stretches of navigable white water. National Park Service rangers present educational programs and hikes, and Grand Canyon Association bookstores make available hundreds of educational titles in book form as well as audio, video, maps, and posters. Tours by bus, train, and air are offered by many sources.

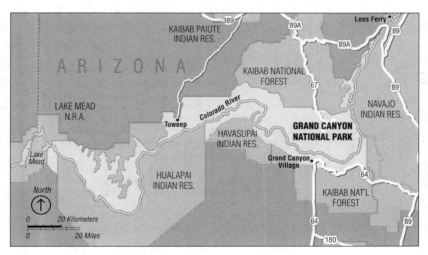

The park incorporates three geographically separated units: the South Rim, North Rim, and inner canyon. The South Rim is the most accessible by all types of transportation and has the most visitors and facilities and services. It is open year round, with the highest concentrations of people from April through September, and the least from November through February. Each season has its appeal. Winter months are cold and trails may be icy, but there are fewer people in the park and inner canyon conditions can be very good. Spring weather is totally unreliable, trailheads may still be snowpacked, but cactus may be blooming in the inner canyon. Summer conditions on the rim are

INTRODUCTION

lovely, but inner canyon heat makes hiking difficult, and there are throngs of visitors. Autumn is beautiful, cooler in the inner canyon, and the crowds thin out somewhat.

The **North Rim** presents a much more tranquil experience. Heavy snowfall closes the area by late October each year; as soon as the road is plowed in the spring, usually by mid-May, the park opens to visitors. It is not served by trains or buses, and the nearest major airports and automobile rental agencies are in Salt Lake City, Utah (380 miles north), and Las Vegas, Nevada (280 miles southwest). The distance from South Rim to North Rim by automobile is 220 miles. On foot, it is a twenty-one-mile cross-canyon hike. The number of visitors is about one-tenth that of the South Rim. The facilities are excellent but limited.

The **inner canyon** can be accessed by foot, mule, or by boat from the Colorado River. Though sixteen established trails enter the Canyon, only the Bright Angel, South Kaibab, and North Kaibab are regularly maintained. Hiking the inner canyon is physically challenging and requires careful planning but can bring rewards of beauty and solitude. All overnight hikes require permits (See Backcountry Permits & Overnight Hiking). From either rim there are numerous below-the-rim day hiking routes, no less difficult than overnight hikes, just shorter. Because all canyon hiking is difficult, any hike, short or long, must be approached with good sense. Please see Day Hikes into the Canyon for trails, preparation, and cautions.

Lees Ferry, at the park's northeastern boundary just off U.S. Highway 89A, is open year round. It is the put-in point for white water raft trips and a favored fishing spot.

Tuweep, 149 miles by road west of the North Rim unit, is reached by a sixty-mile dirt road (impassable when wet) that leaves Highway 389 west near Fredonia, Arizona. Though remote, this park area is becoming more widely known and can be crowded on holiday weekends. Tuweep is open year round.

Within a day's drive of Grand Canyon, there are numerous other national parks and monuments with both cultural and natural history themes. Hualapai, Havasupai, Navajo, Hopi, and Kaibab Paiute Indian Reservations, and Monument Valley Navajo Tribal Park are in the area as well. See Attractions in the Region for highlights, addresses, and telephone numbers.

■ WEATHER & CLIMATE

The Canyon cuts laterally across the side of the Kaibab Uplift, a very large domelike bulge in the earth's crust. The North Rim lies on the high side, 8,100 feet above sea level; the South Rim 1,000 feet lower; between them, the mile-deep Colorado River gorge. The same weather events affect the three areas quite differently because of the widely differing elevations.

The **North Rim** is the coolest and wettest part of the park. About twenty-five inches of precipitation, much of it snow, fall during a year. The rainy season is mid-July to mid-August when thunderstorms come up by early afternoon, bestow brief, and occasionally violent, downpours, then subside until the next afternoon. Lightning is a very real danger (See Safety), and heavy rains can cause flashflooding and trail washouts. If you arrive soon after the North Rim opens for the season in mid-May, there may be snow still on the ground. In September snow may fall off and on; the park closes before the heavy weather begins in November. Sweaters and warm bedding are welcome equipment anytime during the visitor season. During the winter usually more than ten feet of snow will accumulate. In the spring, snowplows begin to clear the road to the park, starting at Jacob Lake and working south, and arrive at their destination about a month later, usually having been beset by additional late spring snowfalls along the way. This process is of great interest among South Rim residents, daily progress reports circulate, and there is a general congratulatory spirit when the job is completed.

Cloaked in snow in winter or radiating heat in summer, Grand Canyon offers vastly different experiences to the visitor.
Photos by George H. H. Huey

The **South Rim** is about 7,100 feet above sea level and receives an average of fifteen inches of precipitation a year. May and June are the driest months. Summer monsoon patterns are the same on both rims and present the same flooding and lightning dangers. Nighttime temperatures are cool even in summer. By mid-September autumn weather approaches, with golden light and daytime highs in the sixties, prevailing into November. Local weather lore says there is usually a dusting of snow for Halloween, and a major snowstorm at Thanksgiving. From the end of December through February it can be very cold, with temperatures dropping near zero at night. The South Rim gets about sixty inches of snow a year. As with the Southwest in general, patterns are erratic. Some years snow falls and melts within a few days; some years snow and icepack remain on the ground all winter. There may be rain in December rather than snow. Spring is more like winter and spring shuffled together than a succession of springlike days. It will not be dependably warm again until June when, overnight, summer arrives.

The **Colorado River** at Phantom Ranch is 2,400 feet above sea level, a mile or so lower than either rim. As you hike down the trail, the climate becomes dryer and hotter. The inner canyon receives a mere

WEATHER & CLIMATE

eight to nine inches of rain a year, and summer high temperatures can be well over one hundred degrees. From the rim you may note clouds over the inner canyon trailing veils of rain that disappear in midair, virga; the raindrops are evaporating before they can reach the canyon floor. Early day Navajo called virga "hairs of the clouds." Rainfall on the canyon rims and surrounding plateau country can cause flash-flooding in tributary canyons. In other words, flashfloods can be a danger even if it is not raining on you (See Safety).

The best preparation for your trip is to bring layers of clothing, shirts, sweaters, and jackets that can be added or removed to maintain a comfortable and safe body temperature. (See Safety for information on the dangers of heat and cold.) A water-repellent outer shell is a good idea any time of the year. In the summer wear a brimmed hat and cover your torso and arms. The sunlight is intense about 350 days a year; wear a hat even in the winter and use sunscreen.

ROAD CONDITIONS

Weather can have a profound effect on your travel plans. During cold-weather months (November through May), check regional road conditions ☎ before you start out. Highways are occasionally closed because of snow, although usually not for more than a few hours at a time, and vehicles may be required to have snowtires or chains.

■ SAFETY

Use Caution Near the Edge.

For your safety, do not climb over guardrails, and use good judgment nearing the edge in all circumstances.

Do not attempt to go below the rim where there is no developed trail.

Hold onto the kids!

ALTITUDE WARNING

The South Rim of Grand Canyon National Park lies at an elevation of about 7,000 feet above sea level; the North Rim, 8,000. Even mild physical exertion at these altitudes can cause breathing or heart problems for some people. Know your limits and do not push yourself.

DANGERS OF HEAT & COLD

Canyon trails will stress the body and all its systems. Day hiking is as difficult as an overnight trek. Don't ask more of your body than it can give. Every year more than a dozen Grand Canyon hikers die of heat-related illness.

Heat exhaustion can be a serious, but generally not life threatening, problem. Early symptoms are very little or no urination, loss of appetite, and loss of thirst, progressing to extreme fatigue, headache, nausea, vomiting, and fainting. Treatment (and prevention) consists of getting out of the heat, frequent periods of rest, drinking plenty of water, and eating nutritious snacks. Recovery can take days.

Heat stroke, on the other hand, is extremely serious and can be life threatening. Early symptoms include illogical behavior, hallucinations, elevated body temperature, flushed appearance, and weak, rapid pulse. Unconsciousness, seizures, and death can follow. The victim must be cooled immediately. Pour water on the victim's head and torso, and fan to create evaporative cooling; move the victim to shade; remove excess clothing. Send someone for help while efforts to cool the victim continue.

Sidestep these unpleasant and critical situations—avoid midday sun; cool off regularly in the shade; wear a hat and shirt (Canyon hiking is not the time to work on your tan!), and use some of your water supply or water from streams to soak your clothing.

Then there is the flip side, cold. Did you know **hypothermia** can occur at temperatures as warm as fifty degrees Fahrenheit? In the Canyon climate, where even in the summer rim temperatures can drop below fifty degrees at night, hypothermia can be a threat year round. In windy and/or wet conditions, a tired hiker can become dangerously chilled. Symptoms include fatigue, drowsiness, uncontrollable shivering, poor muscle control, and careless or illogical behavior; unconsciousness may follow. See that the victim has dry clothing, hot drinks, and protection from wind, rain, and cold. Skin contact with another person can help warm the victim.

During cooler months and late on summer days, stay dry. Wear wind- and water-resistant outer clothing, and dress in layers so garments can be taken off or added as needed. Wool and some synthetic fabrics

SAFETY

wick moisture away from the skin and make good first layers. Eat high-energy foods and drink warm fluids.

GETTING IN SHAPE

I'm not sure there is a way to train for Grand Canyon hiking. Being in basic good physical shape is an advantage, certainly. The relentless downhill trek stresses the knees, upper thighs, hips, and can cause blisters on the toes. The uphill pull attacks the buttocks, calves, and causes blisters on the heels.

You will witness a lot of people who hiked two days ago walking as though their leg joints are fused—it's called the Canyon Shuffle. In addition to this stiff-legged gait, the victim will often have clinched teeth, and will be scanning the landscape for curbs and other insurmountable obstacles.

LIGHTNING

Lightning at Grand Canyon is not a remote statistical possibility; take precautions during electrical storms.

Much of Grand Canyon area's annual precipitation falls during July and August, the "monsoon" season. Typically the day dawns bright and clear, by late morning cumulus clouds gather, becoming towering cumulonimbus giants by early afternoon. The cloud base may be only a few thousand feet above the ground, while its head reaches 60,000 feet, encounters the stratosphere, and spreads into the characteristic anvil shape. Such storms can be quite localized, and often you will witness separate thunderstorms skating across the sky, hurling lightning bolts, reverberating with thunder, and trailing rainfall of varying intensity. Though such storms pass over quickly, usually in fifteen or twenty minutes, rain can fall in torrents and often results in flashflooding.

Lightning kills more people than any other circumstance of weather, with the exception of flashfloods—on average two hundred per year in the United States. All thunderstorms are dangerous and pose a hazard to anyone in open spaces. It would be hard to devise a situation more lightning-luring than being on the canyon rim near a metal guardrail or with your eye to the viewfinder of a camera mounted on a tripod. Don't count on your rubber-soled shoes to help; they do not provide enough insulation to protect a person from lightning.

Lightning at Grand Canyon is not a remote statistical possibility. Strikes have fried numerous telephone systems and computers; El Tovar's flagpole is hit with some regularity; note that the crowns of most of the tallest ponderosa trees have been blown off and their trunks split.

If you can hear thunder, lightning is a danger even if clouds are not directly overhead. Rain does not have to be falling for lightning to strike.

What to Do:

If you are outdoors, hurry to safety at the first flash of lightning. Get indoors if you can.

Avoid hilltops, open spaces, the canyon rim, metal guardrails, or any other electricity conductive object like a tree or a flagpole.

Avoid the highest objects in the area. Never take shelter under a tree. If only isolated trees are nearby, your best protection is to crouch in the open, keeping twice as far away from isolated trees as the trees are tall.

If your hair stands on end or your skin tingles, lightning may be about to strike you. Drop to the ground immediately.

Being in a car is safer than being outside since the metal body will carry the lightning to the ground. Roll up the windows, and do not touch any metal parts of the car.

Lightning can come indoors. When lightning strikes a building, it can flow through plumbing, electrical or telephone wires. During a thunderstorm do not use the telephone or take a bath or shower.

■ ENTRANCE FEES, PERMITS & PASSES

The park entrance fee is $20 per private vehicle, $10 pedestrian or cyclist, payable upon entry to the park. Admission is for seven days, includes both rims, and covers entrance fee only. There are no refunds due to inclement weather. Fees for commercial bus passengers vary.

GOLDEN EAGLE PASSPORT—$50; valid for twelve months from the date of purchase. Available at park entrance stations only, and may be purchased by any United States citizen or permanent resident. Gives access to any National Park Service fee area for passport holder and any accompanying persons in private vehicle; non-transferable and non-refundable; covers entrance fee only.

GOLDEN AGE PASSPORT—$10; lifetime pass available to United States citizens or permanent residents sixty-two years of age or older. May be purchased only at park entrance stations. Gives access to any National Park Service fee area for passport holder and any accompanying persons in private vehicle; non-transferable and non-refundable; covers entrance fees and gives one-half off camping fee at National Park Service campgrounds.

GOLDEN ACCESS PASSPORT—Lifetime pass; free of charge. United States citizens who have a physical, mental, or sensory impairment that substantially limits one or more major life activities may apply in person at any National Park Service information center. Must provide documentation of disability or sign a Statement of Disability. Gives access to any National Park Service fee area for passport holder and any accompanying persons in private vehicle; non-transferable and non-refundable; covers entrance fee and gives one-half off camping fee at National Park Service campgrounds.

HELPFUL FREE PUBLICATIONS

☎ refers you to Address & Telephone listing.

Grand Canyon Trip Planner—Provides up-to-date information, reservation numbers, a list of publications available by mail, and other pertinent material you might need in planning a trip. To receive a copy by mail, contact Grand Canyon National Park ☎.

Backcountry Trip Planner—Permits are mandatory for any overnight hike into the Canyon. This trip planner includes a permit request form, maps, and other critical information as well as a list of hiking guides, maps, and publications available by mail. To receive a copy, contact Grand Canyon National Park ☎.

Accessibility Guide—Contains detailed information on North and South Rim accessibility. Covers parking, overlooks, buildings, and tours. Includes maps. To receive a copy by mail, contact Grand Canyon National Park ☎.

A Quick Look at Grand Canyon National Park—Brief data on the park, its human and natural history; map; suggested reading. To receive a copy by mail, contact Grand Canyon National Park ☎.

THE GUIDE—Up-to-date seasonal information on facilities, services, programs; map. South Rim, North Rim, French, and German language editions are published. Copies are available at all entrance stations, park visitor facilities, and at many other locations within the park.

■ Backcountry Permits & Overnight Hiking

There are sixteen trails and many "routes" in the inner canyon; only the Corridor Trails—the Bright Angel and Kaibab—are maintained and checked regularly by trail crews. None, *none*, **none** of them is easy. The desert climate is extreme in all aspects. Careful planning— enough food and water, the proper clothing to protect you from the elements, deciding the route to take, knowing your physical limits, and what to do in an emergency—can quite literally make a life-or-death difference. About 400 Grand Canyon hikers a year run into significant trouble and must be rescued. Take canyon hiking seriously. Done properly, it can be a glorious, life-changing experience.

You must obtain a permit to camp anywhere in the park other than a developed campground on the rim. This goes for overnight hiking, overnight horseback riding, overnight cross-country ski trips, and overnight off-river hikes by raft trip members. Back-country permits are not required for overnight stays in the dormitories or cabins at Phantom Ranch. However, reservations are required for Phantom Ranch accommodations and meals. See Inner Canyon, Lodging, for more complete information.

Backcountry Office at Maswik Transportation Center in Grand Canyon Village.

Backcountry permits are currently $20 each, plus $4 per person per night backcountry camping fee, and may be obtained up to five months in advance.

Plan trips in advance through the Backcountry Office to be certain you can get reservations for the dates and routes you want. Call or write to Grand Canyon National Park ☎ for a *Backcountry Trip Planner*. This free publication outlines in detail the permit application process and includes a permit request form. Here are some highlights:

In-person applications for future hikes may be made at the South Rim Backcountry Office located at Maswik Transportation Center, open daily all year 8 A.M.– noon, and 1–5 P.M.; or North Rim Backcountry Office, open daily from 8 A.M. to noon, mid-May through October only. Pipe Spring National Monument near Fredonia, Arizona, and the Bureau of Land Management offices in St. George and Kanab, Utah, may issue permits for a limited number of use areas in their vicinities (North Rim).

If you arrive at the park without a backcountry permit and want to hike while you are there, you can put your name on a waiting list by being at the Backcountry Office at 8 A.M. on the day you wish to hike. The *Backcountry Trip Planner* states that you can put your name on the waiting list "for as many consecutive days as are necessary to obtain a permit," a subtle indication of the likelihood of success.

The busiest hiking times are spring and fall months, holidays, and any school vacation period.

The Backcountry Office has an information line ☎ (not a reservation line) which is staffed (not a recording) between 1 P.M. and 5 P.M.

BACKCOUNTRY PERMITS & OVERNIGHT HIKING

Monday through Friday except on federal holidays. Recorded "back-country conditions" message ☎ can be heard by calling on a touch-tone phone. Follow recorded instructions to reach the Backcountry Information menu.

The Backcountry Office does not make reservations for on-rim camp-grounds, river trips, mule trips, Phantom Ranch lodging or meals, or trips to the Havasupai Indian Reservation.

As you consider an inner-canyon hike, backcountry rangers would like you to keep these things in mind:

Make your first overnight hike on one of the Corridor Trails, the Bright Angel, South or North Kaibab. Along these trails lie three developed campgrounds. You can depart from the South Rim any time of the year; from the North Rim only from mid-May to late October.

Try to schedule at least two nights in the Canyon, allowing you to cover less distance in one day or giving you one day and night to recover before you hike out.

A minimum of three nights is recommended to hike rim-to-rim. The distance from the South Rim to the Colorado River is about $7^{1}/_{2}$ miles; from the River Trail Junction to the North Rim, a little over $14^{1}/_{2}$ miles.

Hikes from the South Rim will begin from 7,000 feet above sea level; 8,500 feet on the North Rim. High altitude can have a profound effect on people who live at lower elevations (and most of us do), causing extreme fatigue, dizziness, nausea, headache, and fainting.

Spring and fall are the best times both for safety and enjoyment.

■ GENERAL INFORMATION

FIRE

Lightning ignites about 9,000 forest fires in the United States yearly. Because lightning-started fires have been a fact of life for forests for many millions of years, plant species have adapted to the extent that they not only can survive fire, many depend on a fire cycle for ongoing health. Periodic (the important factor) burning returns

nutrients to the soil and improves its quality and friability, and sustains growth processes; it kills off intruding species that compete with native plants for soil and water; it keeps the amount of burnable material down. Lack of fire not only thwarts the adaptive strategies of forests, it allows excess fuel load to accumulate so that when fire comes, and it will, the damage will be severe.

Trunk scars indicate that historically on the South Rim, forest fires have swept through about every 10 years; forests on the North

Today's park resource managers are prescribing managed burns to reduce fire hazard and restore a natural balance.

Rim, every 70 to 250 years. Trees have various ways of protecting themselves from fire. Pines and firs have thick, spongy bark that is slow to burn and provides good insulation. In some species, as is particularly evident in ponderosas, first branches grow high above the reach of ground fire. The heat of fire opens pine cones, aiding in seed dispersal.

Today's resource managers are taking a fresh look at fire management and are moving away from total suppression of forest and wildland fire as has been attempted for decades. Grand Canyon National Park managers recognize that forest and woodland ecosystems are out of balance because of almost a century of fire suppression, and have initiated a comprehensive strategy to reduce fire hazards and restore natural balance. This includes a "prescribed fire" program in which areas that need to be burned are ignited when wind speed and direction, fuel moisture, potential for smoke dispersal, and forecasted weather conditions are right. Fire managers estimate that 250,000 acres in the park need to be treated, so given the proper conditions, you may well see signs advising of prescribed burns and encounter their smoke during your visit.

DO NOT FEED THE WILDLIFE
Please note that there is no "Please" stated or implied.

Admire the animals, but do not come in contact with them; it can be dangerous for you. As you may have read in your local newspaper, every year Arizona reports cases of bubonic plague, THE Plague, which can be carried by squirrels. Some canyon squirrels are notorious beggars, and they *will* bite the hand that feeds them. Numbers of park visitors are treated at the clinic each season.

Human food and contact are dangerous for the animals as well. When fifteen park deer became so ill that rangers had to shoot them, autopsies were performed in an effort to trace the problem. Every one of these deer had become accustomed to human food and their stomachs were filled with and blocked by food-associated garbage—packaging, plastic bags, string. They could not digest appropriate browse even when they got it; they were starving.

GENERAL INFORMATION

The animals, small and large, you see in the park are not pets, they are not tame. Stay away from them. It is not cute, but cruel, to feed them, and it is illegal.

SOUVENIRS & AMERICAN INDIAN ARTS & CRAFTS

Grand Canyon National Park is in Indian country, near the Havasupai, Hualapai, Navajo, Hopi, and Kaibab Paiute Indian Reservations. Different groups are noted for particular crafts—jewelry, silverwork, weaving, basketry, pottery, wood carving, and sand paintings. Much of the craftsmanship is superb in design and execution. For the most part, shops in the park carry a wide range of American Indian crafts, from exquisitely handcrafted (and priced accordingly) collector items on down the line to mass-reproductions. All are appropriately marked, however, and should leave you with no doubts as to the authenticity and manufacture of products. You will often find that sales personnel are knowledgeable about Indian arts and crafts, and there are numerous books on the subject to which you may wish to refer before you purchase. Aside from learning to recognize good work, you may find many of the methods and individual artists fascinating.

On the Navajo Indian Reservation there are numerous roadside stands operated by American Indians under tribal supervision. Goods are interesting but may be of varying quality.

In almost every reservation community there are established trading posts and cultural centers where extremely well crafted products may be found.

THINGS TO NOTE

Pets must be on-leash at all times and are not allowed on trails below the rim.

Firearms are not allowed in the park unless they are unloaded and broken down.

Wood gathering is not permitted in the park.

PRIVATE STOCK USE IN PARK

The use of private stock in Grand Canyon National Park is permitted. However, before you show up at the park with your horse, write to Grand Canyon National Park ☎ requesting a Private Stock Use Handout for complete information. Information is not available by telephone.

SUNRISE/SUNSET

There is no one "best" place to catch the sunrise or sunset. Check a map for any point that extends out into the Canyon or appears to have open views to the east and/or west. For instance, the hotel area of the South Rim, though not on a peninsula, provides an excellent viewing experience because of its openness. East Rim Drive viewpoints are good for the same reason. Hermits Rest, on the other hand, sits back in the relatively narrow Hermit Creek drainage and doesn't provide a sweeping east-west view.

WEDDINGS

There seem to be a growing number of couples who wish to make their wedding vows at Grand Canyon. If you wish to say "I do," here's what you must do:

- Obtain a marriage license from the State of Arizona. This can be done at any courthouse in the state. The nearest to the South Rim is in Flagstaff or Williams; call the Clerk of the Superior Court ☎. On the North Rim, contact the Justice Court ☎ in Fredonia.

- If you plan to be married outdoors, obtain detailed information and/or a permit by writing to Wedding Permit Information, Grand Canyon National Park ☎. With your request include: the exact date and time of the event, how many people will be present, the location you are requesting, and who will be performing the ceremony. The park requires this information in advance and in writing.

- Arrange for someone to perform the ceremony. This can be a Justice of the Peace or a licensed minister. Contact them in advance to inquire about fees and to set a time. The park can provide a list of names and telephone numbers.

Outdoor weddings require a permit (it is free) from the park. Some viewpoints—but not all—are available for weddings, and only one (Shoshone Point) may be used for receptions. The park has one indoor facility (the Shrine of the Ages) which may be reserved in advance. There is a fee for use of indoor park facilities and Shoshone Point.

Indoor ceremonies and receptions at Grand Canyon National Park Lodges ☎ facilities do not require permits. Contact them in advance to make arrangements for space and catering or for information on fees.

DAYS OF THE YEAR BUSINESSES & FACILITIES ARE CLOSED

Federal Holidays (bank, post office, backcountry office phones closed) Check a current calendar to note when holidays are actually observed:

New Year's Day
Martin Luther King Jr.'s Birthday
Presidents' Day
Memorial Day
Independence Day
Labor Day
Columbus Day
Veterans' Day
Thanksgiving Day
Christmas Day

Babbitt's General Store: Thanksgiving Day, Christmas Day, New Year's Day

The South Rim of Grand Canyon National Park, the Visitor Center, and Grand Canyon National Park Lodges facilities are open every day of the year.

GENERAL INFORMATION

The North Rim of Grand Canyon National Park, its NPS information and visitor facilities, and Grand Canyon Lodge facilities are open mid-May through late October only. See North Rim, Seasonal Activities for winter use information.

WORLD HERITAGE SITE

The World Heritage Convention, which promotes worldwide cooperation in preserving places of universal natural and cultural significance, has to date named 469 World Heritage Sites. Among them are the Taj Mahal in India, England's Westminster Abbey, the Pyramids of Egypt, and the Great Wall of China.

Grand Canyon was awarded World Heritage Site status in 1979. A plaque was mounted in the South Rim Visitor Center courtyard at the dedication ceremony.

CANYON NIGHTS

Hundreds of miles from big city light pollution, the night sky at Grand Canyon is a marvel. The full moon, aside from its breathtaking rise, shines so brightly it casts hard shadows among inner canyon formations. During the dark of the moon or new moon times, the stars burn like perfect diamonds in a bottomless black universe, and the Milky Way is like a glowing brushstroke.

To describe the park as "dark" during moonless nights would be an understatement. It is dark in the extreme, and there are few streetlights. You can barely see your hand in front of your face, much less the trail or sidewalk. Carry a flashlight with you at all times.

TRAINS AT GRAND CANYON

Railroads were instrumental in early development of tourism at both rims of Grand Canyon. The Atchison, Topeka and Santa Fe Railway, building their way to the west coast, laid tracks fifty miles south of Grand Canyon in 1883. In 1901 the railway bought from a defunct copper mining company track running north from Williams. The

First train to carry passengers to Grand Canyon, 1901.

Grand Canyon Railway Company, a subsidiary of the AT&SF, completed the track to the canyon rim, and the first passenger train arrived on September 17, 1901. For many years most tourists arrived at Grand Canyon by train, but growing use of private automobiles on an ever-improving highway system caused dwindling numbers of riders, and in 1968 the last passenger train pulled away from the Grand Canyon depot.

In 1989 the romance of the rails was revived when the Grand Canyon Railway, a privately owned company, amid great celebration brought its first passenger train to the rim. Steam engines, built in 1906 and 1910, and 1950s-vintage diesel locomotives pull authentically restored 1923 Harriman coach cars on daily runs. The 131,000 passengers arriving by train means that about 46,000 fewer automobiles enter the park annually. See Commercial Tours, South Rim.

Although the Union Pacific Railroad ran to Cedar City, Utah, about 165 miles north of the park, the first director of the park service, Stephen Mather, encouraged the company to provide transportation and accommodations on the North Rim. In 1927 their subsidiary, Utah Parks Company, began to offer daily bus service and mule trips. The railroad built the Grand Canyon Lodge and 120 cabins at Bright Angel Point, and a powerhouse and pumping plant at Roaring Springs to provide water to the rim. In 1971, when the Union Pacific halted passenger operations, it donated all of its North Rim facilities to the National Park Service.

THE FRED HARVEY COMPANY

The Atchison, Topeka and Santa Fe Railway's line reached from Kansas to the Pacific by 1883. It crept across prairies, plains and deserts where settlement was sparse to absent, and trains stopped at mining and cattle camps, boom towns, and remote government installations, most of which had the poorest of lodgings and meals. In the absence of hotels, a cot in a public room might be the only option for sleeping arrangements. Saloons often provided the only food, generally of terrible quality, on stops that were often too brief for customers to finish the meal. Seasoned travelers might leave home with a supply of food; however, long before arriving at their destination, it would have given out or become unfit to eat.

Fred Harvey buses on El Tovar Hill about 1922.

Fred Harvey, a young English emigrant, gained first-hand experience with poor traveling conditions as a railroad employee who spent time on the rails. Harvey convinced the Atchison, Topeka and Santa Fe Railway to give him a small restaurant in the Topeka, Kansas, depot. Harvey's high standards for food and facilities soon earned an excellent reputation. The Topeka restaurant became so popular that passengers ". . . positively declined to go further once they had eaten with Fred Harvey." The railway, realizing the advertising advantage of good food, encouraged Harvey to open additional restaurants along their line. Harvey Houses, with food brought in by the railroad, provided fine, fresh food and exquisite linens and silver where no one else could. "Fred Harvey Meals All the Way" became a railway slogan. Throughout their long relationship, the railway built and owned the hotels and restaurants that Fred Harvey managed, and, in fact, subsidized his operations, which consistently lost money.

Harvey's ventures expanded to include gift shops and tours. He hired architect Mary Colter in 1902. For forty years she designed and decorated Harvey's hotels and shops throughout the Southwest, including Bright Angel Lodge, Lookout Studio, Hopi House, Hermits Rest, Watchtower, Phantom Ranch, and the interior of El Tovar Hotel.

■ THE SOUTH RIM— GETTING THERE

View of the Canyon from Grandview Point on the East Rim Drive. Photo by George H. H. Huey

Grand Canyon National Park's South Rim has two developed areas, twenty-five miles apart. Grand Canyon Village is westernmost and is the location of most park facilities and service. Desert View is at the park's east entrance station and has limited facilities and services, many of which are open only seasonally.

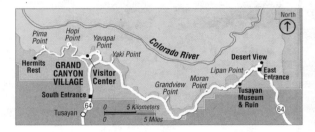

In this guidebook and other literature you will see references to the East Rim and the West Rim. Since you are well aware that the Canyon has north and south rims, this may lead you to ponder whether the Canyon is square. It is not. An east/west road runs along the South Rim from Desert View to Hermits Rest, the westernmost viewpoint accessible by paved road on the South Rim. From Desert View west to the junction with the South Entrance Road, it is known as East Rim Drive. From the West Rim Interchange near the Bright Angel Lodge to Hermits Rest it is known as West Rim Drive.

BY CAR

State Highway 64 runs through the park's South Rim unit, providing access to entrance stations on its south and east boundaries.

SOUTH ENTRANCE STATION—From Interstate 40, State Highway 64 may be approached from Williams or Flagstaff, Arizona. From Williams, State Highway 64, a fairly straight but hilly two-lane road, goes fifty miles north to the park. Most of the way it runs through

sagebrush/desertscrub, but there is some ponderosa and pinyon-juniper forest. Along the way are limited gas stations, commercial campgrounds, restaurants, and other accommodations. Automobile, bus, and RV traffic is heavy. Use extreme caution at all times. In cold months the road may be icy and snowpacked. Check road conditions ☎ before you leave Williams.

From Flagstaff, take U.S. Highway 180 fifty miles to its juncture with State Highway 64, and from there another twenty-eight miles to the park. Highway 180 is two-lane with many curves and hills and very little shoulder. Much of its course winds through ponderosa forest, opening to pinyon-juniper, and then sagebrush/desertscrub. No services are available between Flagstaff and the Highway 64 junction. Winter storms occasionally require the road to be closed, but there may not be advisory signs until you get to the roadblock several miles out of town. If there is snow, check road conditions ☎ before you leave Flagstaff. The distance from Flagstaff to the park via Highway 180 is eighty miles. Automobile, bus, and RV traffic is heavy. Use extreme caution at all times.

Both of the southern approaches are situated in a distinctly volcanic landscape, from the three majestic San Francisco Peaks—Humphreys Peak (12,670 feet), Kendrick Peak (10,418 feet), and Agassiz Peak (12,356 feet)—to the gracefully shaped cinder cones that dot the countryside. A few miles north of the junction of highways 180 and 64 Red Butte (an erosional remnant rather than a volcanic structure) stands alone on the east side of the road.

Just south of the entrance station is the community of Tusayan, where information, lodging, food, camping, fuel, tour operations, and other services are provided (See Facilities and Services Outside the Park). Grand Canyon Airport is adjacent to Tusayan.

THE SOUTH RIM—GETTING THERE

SOUTH ENTRANCE STATION—Most visitors to the park arrive at the south entrance station and proceed seven miles on a two-lane road through pinyon-juniper and ponderosa forest toward the rim and Grand Canyon Village, the location of most of the park's facilities and services. Two roads turn off the main entrance road. Center Road, on which the clinic and various park administrative facilities are located, goes west off the main entrance road; unless your destination is one of those facilities, stay on the main road. The East Rim Drive (State Highway 64) turns east to run twenty-five miles to Desert View and the park's east entrance station.

EAST ENTRANCE STATION—To enter the park from the east, turn west onto State Highway 64 from U.S. Highway 89 near Cameron, Arizona, on the Navajo Indian Reservation, which is governed by the tribe according to tribal rules and regulations, including speed limits. There are gas stations and limited food services in and around Cameron. There are no facilities or services on the thirty-mile stretch from the junction of highways 64 and 89 to the park entrance. If there is snow, check road conditions ☎ before you travel. State Highway 64 is two-lane with hills and curves and runs through desert scrub and pinyon-juniper forest. Automobile, bus, and RV traffic is heavy. Use extreme caution at all times.

Eastern views allow amazing open panoramas, the Vermilion and Echo Cliffs, and on a clear day, Navajo Mountain.

NOTE: "Open seasonally" generally means May through September.

At the east entrance is Desert View. It provides a gas station (open seasonally), Babbitt's General Store, Trading Post fountain and gift shop, the Watchtower and gift shop, and NPS Information Center. A campground is open seasonally.

The twenty-five-mile stretch of the East Rim Drive from Desert View west to Grand Canyon Village runs parallel with the canyon rim through pinyon-juniper and ponderosa forest. The two-lane road is curved and hilly with very little shoulder. In cold weather the road can be treacherous.

The major overlooks along the East Rim Drive are Lipan, Moran, Grandview, and Yaki Points, all with clearly marked turn-offs (See Overlooks). There are numerous beside-the-road pullouts where you may take in the vista. Park only at designated pullouts, never on the road shoulder. Drive carefully; vehicle operators may be distracted by the scenery.

A great deal of thought has been given to informational signs within the park. However, the developed area is large and not gridlike, so you will probably need to refer to maps frequently to get your bearings. The good news is if you stay on the main roads you really cannot become permanently lost.

BY AIR

The nearest airports with scheduled airline service are Flagstaff, Arizona (80 miles southeast), Phoenix, Arizona (220 miles south), and Las Vegas, Nevada (220 miles west). There is limited service to Grand

Canyon Airport (seven miles south of the park) from Las Vegas and elsewhere. Check with a travel agent for further information.

BY BUS

Greyhound Bus Lines ☎ has scheduled service to Flagstaff and Williams, Arizona, from points nationwide. Service connecting to Grand Canyon can be made through Gray Line of Flagstaff Nava-Hopi Tours. ☎ Fares for connecting service are not included in any Greyhound Bus Lines passes or fares.

Gray Line of Flagstaff Nava-Hopi Tours ☎ offers scheduled service between Grand Canyon, Flagstaff, and Williams, Arizona. Call Gray Line of Flagstaff Nava-Hopi Tours or check with Grand Canyon National Park Lodges transportation desks in the park for schedule.

BY TRAIN

AMTRAK ☎ provides scheduled service to Flagstaff, Arizona. Connecting bus service to Grand Canyon is available through Gray Line of Flagstaff Nava-Hopi Tours ☎.

Grand Canyon Railway ☎ runs excursion trains from Williams, Arizona, to the Canyon daily except December 24 and 25. Three classes of service are offered with round-trip adult fares ranging from $49 to $99 per person, children from $19 to $69. Trains depart Williams at 9:30 A.M., arrive at Grand Canyon at 11:45 A.M.; depart Grand Canyon at 3:15 P.M., arrive at Williams at 5:30 P.M. Overnight packages and the option of taking the train one way and a bus back are also available. Prices are subject to change. Write or call for brochures and full information.

CAR RENTAL

Major rental agencies serve Phoenix, Flagstaff, and Las Vegas. Budget Car Rental ☎ maintains a rental desk year round at the Grand Canyon Airport.

■ GRAND CANYON VILLAGE

WHERE TO FIND INFORMATION

NATIONAL PARK SERVICE VISITOR CONTACT STATIONS— NOTE on hours of operation: The following NPS information and visitor centers have in the past operated on extended summer hours. This may not continue as park budgets shrink; however, you can count on their being open from 8 A.M. to 5 P.M. at any time of the year.

Yavapai Observation Station—Located at Yavapai Point, ³/₄ mile east of NPS Visitor Center. Orientation and park information available; ranger-led programs; exhibits; bookstore; glass-enclosed building allows panoramic views of the Canyon, including the Colorado River and Phantom Ranch. Open daily. Restrooms open year round. Drinking water not available in winter months.

NPS Visitor Center—Located six miles north of the south entrance station and twenty-five miles west of the park's east entrance station. Orientation and park information, maps, brochures, exhibit hall with special and standing exhibits, audio-visual program, ranger-led activities, bookstore. Open daily. Restrooms/water.

Kolb Studio—Located in the Village Historic District at the Bright Angel trailhead. This historic structure was begun in 1904 and enlarged periodically through 1926 by pioneer Grand Canyon photographers Emery and Ellsworth Kolb. The public is encouraged to visit the auditorium, where art exhibits are often scheduled. Admission is free. Orientation and park information, brochures, maps, ranger-led activities, bookstore. Open daily.

Backcountry Office—Located at Maswik Transportation Center. Inner canyon hiking information and permits; permits for at-large camping on the rim. Open daily 8 A.M.–noon and 1–5 P.M.

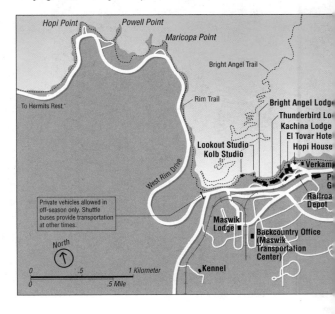

LODGING

For all advance in-park lodging reservations or information contact AMFAC Parks & Resorts ☎.

As a rule, lodging is booked well in advance. If you arrive at the park without room reservations, you may be disappointed and greatly inconvenienced. Call Grand Canyon National Park Lodges ☎ to check on same-day reservations. If there are no cancellations available, you can seek lodging in Tusayan, Valle, Williams, Flagstaff, or Cameron (See Facilities & Services Outside the Park). There are campgrounds in the park, also highly sought after (See Camping), and on forest service land surrounding the park (See Facilities & Services Outside the Park). In-park lodging prices range from about $35 to $275 per night plus applicable taxes. Prices change periodically and those given here should be viewed as ranges only rather than firm costs.

EL TOVAR HOTEL

On the rim, Historic District; rooms, suites, fine dining, lounge, gift shop, newsstand, concierge.

El Tovar was completed in 1905 by the Santa Fe Railway. Architect Charles F. Whittlesey combined design elements of the Swiss chateau and "castles of the Rhine," using native boulders and Douglas-fir logs and boards. The hotel was named for the Spanish explorer Pedro de Tovar, who had visited Hopi Indian villages in 1540, although he did not make it to the Canyon. This elegant building has been beautifully maintained and exudes the graciousness of its early days. It is on the National Register of Historic Places.

THUNDERBIRD LODGE

On the rim; lodging rooms only; check-in at Bright Angel Lodge.

KACHINA LODGE

On the rim; lodging rooms only; check-in at El Tovar Hotel.

These two lodges were built by the Fred Harvey Company in 1968 and 1971 respectively and reflect architectural lines of that particular time.

BRIGHT ANGEL LODGE

On the rim, Historic District; rooms, cabins, restaurant, Arizona Steakhouse, ice cream fountain, bar, gift shop, beauty salon, transportation desk; check-in for Phantom Ranch lodging and meals, and mule rides.

The rustic Bright Angel Lodge was designed by Mary Colter and opened in 1935. In its Canyon Room is a "geological" fireplace, a "rim-to-rim"

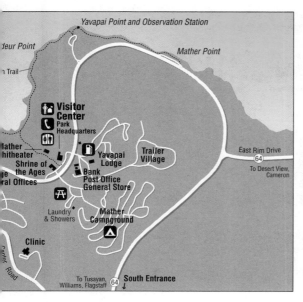

GRAND CANYON VILLAGE

Designed by Mary Colter, the Bright Angel Lodge opened in 1935.

representation of the Canyon built of rock selected by park naturalists to accurately represent each geologic layer, and carried out of the Canyon by mules. Ms. Colter designed and supervised its construction.

MASWIK LODGE

West of Historic District, ¹/₄ mile from rim; rooms, cafeteria, sports bar, gift shop, transportation desk.

Maswik Lodge has a large modern registration lobby/ gift shop/cafeteria/bar building and numerous modern two-story motel-type lodging buildings. It is an easy ten-minute walk from the rim, and the Maswik Transportation Center is just across the street from the registration building.

YAVAPAI LODGE

Near NPS Visitor Center, ¹/₂ mile from rim; rooms, cafeteria, gift shop, transportation desk. Lodge closed from December 1 until March with the exception of December 25 through January 1.

Yavapai Lodge consists of a modern registration lobby/ gift shop/cafeteria building and numerous modern two-story motel-type buildings. It is located near the NPS Visitor Center, Babbitt's General Store, post office, and bank. It is an easy fifteen-minute walk from the rim.

PHANTOM RANCH

See Inner Canyon Lodging.

CAMPING

In the park, camping is permitted only in established campgrounds or at-large in designated sites with a backcountry permit (See Backcountry Permits & Overnight Hiking). Prices given are subject to change.

MATHER CAMPGROUND—Near NPS Visitor Center. NPS-operated campground. Water and restrooms (accessible) available. Six accessible sites. NOTE: As of late 1997 sites in this campground are available on a first-come-first-served basis. This is a temporary arrangement; park managers expect to have a reservation system in place within a few months. To check on the availability of camping reservations at the time of your trip, contact the park for the current *GUIDE*, which will contain up-to-date information. Campgrounds fill early; try to arrive before 10 A.M. to have the best chance for a site.

326 individual tent and RV sites (no hook-ups); $12 per site per day; maximum two vehicles and six people per site.

Seven group sites; $39.95 per day; maximum five vans or two tour buses.

TRAILER VILLAGE—Near NPS Visitor Center. Concessioner-operated campground. Make reservations through AMFAC Parks & Resorts ☎. Open year round.

Eighty RV sites with hook-ups (water, electric, sewer); restrooms; no shower facilities; $18 per site per day for two people, $1.75 for each additional person.

LAUNDRY & SHOWERS—Near Mather Campground. Coin-operated laundry open daily 7 A.M.–9 P.M.; last wash load at 7:45 P.M. Coin-operated showers available daily 7 A.M.–9 P.M. Accessible restroom with shower. Open year round.

SANITARY DUMP STATION—Near Mather Campground and Trailer Village. In service mid-May through mid-October.

DINING & FOOD SERVICE

EL TOVAR DINING ROOM ☎— El Tovar Hotel, fine dining; breakfast 6:30–11 A.M.; lunch 11:30 A.M.–2 P.M.; dinner 5–10 P.M. Call for dinner reservations. Lounge open daily 11 A.M.–midnight. Moderate to expensive.

BRIGHT ANGEL RESTAURANT—Bright Angel Lodge; open daily 6 A.M.–11 P.M. Moderate.

ARIZONA STEAKHOUSE—Adjoining Bright Angel Lodge; open daily for dinner only 5–10 P.M. Moderate.

MASWIK CAFETERIA—Maswik Lodge; open daily 6 A.M.–10 P.M. Inexpensive.

YAVAPAI CAFETERIA—Yavapai Lodge; hours 6 A.M.–10 P.M. Closed December 1 until March with the exception of December 25 through January 1. Inexpensive.

GRAND CANYON VILLAGE

BABBITT'S DELICATESSEN—Babbitt's General Store; hours 8 A.M.–6 P.M. Closed Thanksgiving Day, Christmas Day, New Year's Day. Inexpensive.

BRIGHT ANGEL FOUNTAIN—Bright Angel Lodge; hours 6 A.M.–8 P.M. Closed November through March. Inexpensive.

OTHER SERVICES

BANK—Bank One, Grand Canyon Village, next to post office, across from NPS Visitor Center. Open Monday–Thursday 10 A.M.–3 P.M.; Friday 10 A.M.–3 P.M. and 4–6 P.M. Closed Saturday, Sunday and holidays. Will cash traveler's checks and exchange foreign currency. Cash advances on charge cards and wire transfers are available. A twenty-four-hour automated teller machine accepts cards from Bank One, American Express, Plus and Star systems, Arizona Interchange Network, and Master Teller.

BEAUTY & BARBER SHOP—Bright Angel Hair Design ☎, Bright Angel Lodge. Open Tuesday–Saturday 9 A.M.–5 P.M.; additional hours by appointment.

FUEL—Chevron Service Station, near the NPS Visitor Center; gasoline, diesel, propane. Open daily April through October 6 A.M.–9:30 P.M.; other dates 8 A.M.–7 P.M.

GARAGE ☎—Located just east of Grand Canyon National Park Lodges General Offices. Mechanic on duty 8 A.M.–noon and 1–5 P.M. daily. Twenty-four-hour emergency service available. AAA authorized.

GROCERY & GENERAL STORE—Babbitt's General Store, near NPS Visitor Center. Hours 8 A.M.–7 P.M.; closed Thanksgiving Day, Christmas Day, and New Year's Day. Groceries (including meats and produce); Arizona fishing licenses; camping supplies; clothing; souvenirs; delicatessen.

HIKING & CAMPING EQUIPMENT—Babbitt's General Store sells, rents, and does limited repairs on camping, hiking, and backpacking equipment; instep crampon rental and sales; rents cross-country ski equipment; Arizona fishing licenses. Hours 8 A.M. to 7 P.M.; closed Thanksgiving Day, Christmas Day, New Year's Day.

LAUNDRY & SHOWERS—Near Mather Campground. Coin-operated laundry open daily 7 A.M.–9 P.M.; last wash load at 7:45 P.M. Coin-operated showers available daily 7 A.M.–9 P.M.

LOST & FOUND ☎—For items lost or found in lodges, restaurants, or lounges, call Grand Canyon National Park Lodges ☎. For all other lost and found items, call Grand Canyon National Park Lost and Found ☎ between the hours of 8 A.M. and 6:30 P.M.

MEDICAL SERVICES—For twenty-four-hour emergency medical service, call 911. From hotel rooms, dial 9 - 911.

Grand Canyon Clinic ☎ (See Grand Canyon Village map) is open Monday–Friday 8 A.M.– 5:30 P.M. Saturday 9 A.M.–noon. Closed Sundays.

Pharmacy ☎ (See Grand Canyon Village map) hours are Monday–Friday 8:30 A.M.– 12:30 P.M. and 1:30–5:30 P.M. Closed Saturday and Sunday.

Dentist ☎ (See Grand Canyon Village map) is open Monday–Wednesday 8 A.M.–3 P.M.

PET KENNELS—(See Grand Canyon Village map) Boarding reservations are suggested. Proof of vaccination required. Call Grand Canyon National Park Lodges ☎ for information. Hours: daily 7:30 A.M.–5 P.M.; for after hours retrieval, contact Grand Canyon National Park Lodges Fire and Safety Department ☎. Pets must be on a leash at all times in the park and are not allowed below the rim, in park lodges, or on park buses.

POST OFFICE—Grand Canyon Village, across the road from NPS Visitor Center. Window service Monday–Friday 9 A.M.–4:30 P.M. all year, extended to include Saturday and Sunday 10 A.M.–2 P.M. from early May until September. Closed holidays. Stamps available from machine in lobby. Lobby open daily 5 A.M.–10 P.M.

SANITARY DUMP STATION—Near Mather Campground and Trailer Village. In service mid-May through mid-October.

TELEGRAPH & WESTERN UNION—Located in Grand Canyon National Park Lodges General Offices (See Grand Canyon Village map). Open daily 8 A.M.–5 P.M.

WORSHIP SERVICES—Religious services are held in the park. Schedules are posted at Mather Campground, NPS Visitor Center, Shrine of the Ages, and the information kiosk near the post office. The National Park Service does not endorse any group or message.

■ DESERT VIEW

WHERE TO FIND INFORMATION

The Watchtower at Desert View. Photo by George H. H. Huey

NATIONAL PARK SERVICE VISITOR CONTACT STATIONS

Desert View Information Center—Located at the park's east entrance; orientation and park information available; bookstore. Restrooms/water nearby. Open daily 9 A.M.–5 P.M. from May through October.

Tusayan Museum—Three miles west of Desert View; orientation and park information available; bookstore; exhibits; ranger-led programs; self-guiding trail through 800-year-old ancestral Pueblo Indian village and fields. No admission fee. Chemical toilets/water. Open daily 9 A.M.–5 P.M.

LODGING

No lodging facilities are available at Desert View.

CAMPING

DESERT VIEW CAMPGROUND—NPS-operated campground. Self-registration; open mid-May through mid-October; no reservations may be made; sites are available on a first-come-first-served basis. Water and toilets available.

Fifty sites (no hook-ups and no showers); $10 per site per day; maximum two vehicles and six people per site. Accessible restroom, but no designated accessible campsite.

No group site available.

DINING & FOOD SERVICE

TRADING POST FOUNTAIN—April through October open 9 A.M.–10 P.M.; other months 9 A.M.–8 P.M. Cafeteria service. Inexpensive.

OTHER SERVICES

FUEL—Chevron Service Station open seasonally, late March through October; gasoline only, no diesel or propane. Open 8 A.M.– 5 P.M. in spring and fall, 7 A.M.– 7 P.M. during June, July, and August.

GROCERIES & SUPPLIES—Babbitt's General Store; April through October 7 A.M.–7 P.M.; other months 8 A.M.–5 P.M.; closed Thanksgiving Day, Christmas Day, New Year's Day. Groceries (including meats and produce); camping supplies; clothing; souvenirs, United States postage stamps.

WATCHTOWER (See Park Buildings & Landmarks)—Gift shop and tour of historic Watchtower; April through October hours 8 A.M.–7 P.M.; other months 9 A.M.–5 P.M. 25 cent fee for the Watchtower tour.

■ FACILITIES & SERVICES OUTSIDE THE PARK

WHERE TO FIND INFORMATION

Kaibab National Forest, Tusayan Ranger District ☎

LODGING

CAMERON—One mile north of Highways 64 and 89 junction; about 50 miles east of Desert View.

Cameron Trading Post & Motel ☎
Open year round

VALLE—At junction of Highways 64 and 180; about 25 miles south of the park.

Grand Canyon Day's Inn Motel ☎
Open February through November

Grand Canyon Motel
Open May through October; operates on first-come-first-served basis. Check-in at Grand Canyon Day's Inn

TUSAYAN—Near the south entrance station. Most businesses open year round.

Grand Canyon Squire Inn ☎
Holiday Inn Express ☎
Moqui Lodge ☎
Quality Inn ☎
Red Feather Lodge ☎
Seven Mile Lodge ☎

OTHER SERVICES IN TUSAYAN

Restaurants, grocery store, fuel, automatic banking machine, gift shops, IMAX theater, helicopter tours, riding stables. The Grand Canyon Airport is just south of Tusayan. Automobile rental desks are on the premises, as are air and helicopter tour operators.

CAMPING

The United States Forest Service operates **TEN-X CAMPGROUND** two miles south of Tusayan. The campground is open May 1 through September 30. Picnic tables, fire ring, barbecue grill, water, toilets. No showers, no hook-ups, and no reservations. It fills early in the day. Prices are subject to change.

Seventy individual camping sites (most are pull-through car and trailer sites); $10 per site, maximum two vehicles and eight people per site.

Group site ($25 minimum non-refundable fee) for up to one hundred people; reservations are required and may be made by calling the Kaibab National Forest, Tusayan Ranger District ☎.

CAMPER VILLAGE ☎ is a privately operated RV and tent camping facility in Tusayan. 200 sites. Fees range from $15 per day for one tent with two people to $23 per day for trailer space with hook-ups including water, electric, and sewer. Pay showers are available. Toilets, water, dump station, picnic tables, general store, commercial food service, miniature golf. Open year round. Prices are subject to change.

DISPERSED CAMPING ON USFS LAND—The forest service allows camping outside of campgrounds on forest service land. As no facilities will be provided *you must bring your own water*. Regulations are as follows:

- Carry out all of your trash.
- Bury all human waste at least four to six inches deep, a minimum of one hundred feet from water and drainage bottoms.
- Camp at least ¹/₄ mile away from the highway or surface water.
- Camp ¹/₂ mile from developed campgrounds.
- Do not camp in meadows.
- Do not camp within one mile of Hull Cabin.
- Do not camp at Red Butte (between State Highway 64 and Forest Roads 305 and 320).
- Do not dump any waste from RVs—not even gray water.
- Eliminate all signs of your campsite.

For open fires:

- Select a safe place for your open fire. Build your fire on level ground away from steep slopes, rotten logs, stumps, dense dry grass, and litter.
- Clear a circle to bare dirt, being sure to remove all burnable material.
- Keep your fire small and in a shallow pit or fire pan.
- Do not build a fire on a windy day.
- Do not leave fire unattended at any time. To do so violates state and federal laws.
- Put your fire out cold before you leave. Let the fire burn down, separate the embers, mix and stir the coals with dirt and water. Make certain the fire is out by feeling it with your hands. Never bury a fire to put it out. It can escape from under the dirt. Keep mixing and stirring water into the coals until the ashes are cold to the touch.

■ GETTING AROUND IN THE PARK

ON FOOT—The Rim Trail, which is paved from Yavapai Point to Maricopa Point and unpaved on to Hermits Rest, a total distance of almost nine miles, offers a splendid outdoor experience. Much of it is fairly level, but there are inclines near the junction with the NPS Visitor Center trail. From the West Rim Interchange west it is not wheelchair accessible because of steps and steep grades. The trail can be icy and snowpacked in winter months.

Please stay on the paved paths and do not shortcut through the forest. In the region's arid climate trampling of the landscape can take decades to heal.

BICYCLE—In Arizona bicycles must abide by the same traffic rules as automobiles. Bicycles are not allowed on unpaved park roads, any park trails, or on or below the rim. Motor vehicle traffic is heavy on park roads and shoulders are narrow. Use extreme caution when riding in the park. In the summer the West Rim Drive is closed to most private automobile traffic but has heavy bus use, so watch for wide vehicles on this narrow road, and please do not obstruct traffic. There is no bicycle rental available in the park.

The Tusayan Ranger District of the Kaibab National Forest which adjoins the park to the south has numerous routes suitable for mountain bikes. Visit their ranger station in Tusayan to pick up maps and general information.

AUTOMOBILE—Automobile traffic in the park during peak visitation times can be quite astounding, but driving around is not as hard as parking. Parking lots and pullouts are clearly marked. Do not park elsewhere. A recent research poll revealed that, even with almost five million visitors annually to the park, visitors don't feel there are too many people, but rather to many cars. When it is available, use the free shuttle bus and avoid the headaches. At the newly constructed Maswik Transportation Center (See Grand Canyon Village map) there is a large parking lot with shuttle bus service from mid-March through mid-October.

FREE IN-PARK SHUTTLE BUS—From mid-March through mid-October, the park provides transportation by free shuttle bus service. This is a transportation shuttle, not a tour. Stops are clearly marked and have orientation maps. Park management plans to extend shuttle service, both in season and area of coverage, over the next few years. Check *THE GUIDE* for current information. There are three shuttle routes:

West Rim Loop buses depart from the West Rim Interchange, just west of Bright Angel Lodge, at fifteen-minute intervals. Check *THE GUIDE* for current schedules. Going west to Hermits Rest, buses stop at eight overlooks. Returning buses stop only at Mohave Point. Passengers may get on and off buses at any designated stop.

Village Loop buses run at fifteen-minute intervals between Yavapai Observation Station, NPS Visitor Center, hotels, restaurants, campgrounds, and other facilities in the Village area. Check *THE GUIDE* for current schedules.

Yaki Point/South Kaibab Trailhead buses run about every half hour, from sunrise until sunset.

NOTE: The West Rim and Yaki Point/South Kaibab Trailhead are closed to most private vehicles from mid-March through mid-October. The in-park shuttle bus system provides the only transportation to those locations during that period of time.

Shuttle buses do not go to Desert View.

TRANSPORTATION BETWEEN THE PARK, TUSAYAN, AND AIRPORT—Check with Grand Canyon National Park Lodges transportation desks for schedules and fares.

TAXI ☎—Service available to airport, trailheads, and other destinations; twenty-four hours daily. Call for pick up.

TRANSCANYON SHUTTLE ☎—Daily round-trip transportation between the South and North Rims from mid-May through mid-October. Departs the North Rim at 7 A.M., arrives South Rim at noon; departs the South Rim at 1:30 P.M., arrives North Rim at 6:30 P.M. Reservations are necessary. Call Transcanyon Shuttle or contact a Grand Canyon National Park Lodges transportation desk for information and reservations. Fare per person is $60 one way/$100 round trip. Group rates for 10 or more people. Prices subject to change.

The *Grand Canyon National Park Accessibility Guide*, which indicates the accessibility of most public buildings and park facilities and trails, is available free upon request at any NPS information center or by writing Grand Canyon National Park ☎. See Addresses and Telephone Numbers for TDD listing.

SERVICES FOR SPECIAL POPULATIONS

Programs, facilities, and services in the park that are fully or marginally accessible to persons with physical disabilities are noted throughout the free visitor information publication, *THE GUIDE*, with the following symbol: ♿. *THE GUIDE* is available at many locations throughout the park, including all park information centers and museums.

United States citizens who have a physical, mental, or sensory impairment may apply in person at the NPS Visitor Center for a Golden Access Passport. These lifetime permits are free (See Entrance Fees, Permits, & Passes), and they provide entrance to any National Park Service site.

The National Park Service provides, at no charge, wheelchairs for temporary use by park visitors. Check at the NPS Visitor Center information desk. Temporary permits for designated parking may be obtained at the NPS Visitor Center, Kolb Studio, or Yavapai Observation Station.

Wheelchair-accessible tours are available by prior arrangement. Contact any Grand Canyon National Park Lodges transportation desk or call Grand Canyon National Park Lodges ☎ for information. TDD telephones are available in the park to hotel guests.

■ ACTIVITIES

Attend ranger-led programs. NPS rangers give talks and guide walks throughout the year. The schedules change seasonally. Evening programs are held every night at either the Mather Amphitheater or Shrine of the Ages, depending upon the season. Check *THE GUIDE* for current schedules. It is free and can be picked up at any NPS information center and most hotel lobbies. Also, the bulletin board in the NPS Visitor Center entranceway will list topics.

Talks and guided walks are offered by the National Park Service year round.

Experience the audio-visual program in the auditorium of the NPS Visitor Center. Topics and times are posted at the auditorium entrance.

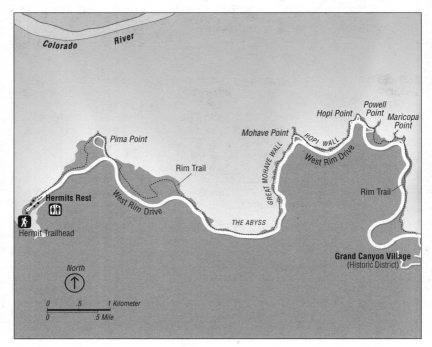

Pick up a *Junior Ranger* publication for kids at any NPS visitor information facility. It includes information, activities, and instructions on how to become a Junior Ranger.

Stop by Yavapai Observation Station. You can take in spectacular canyon views (from indoors!), including Phantom Ranch and the Colorado River. There are special exhibits and a bookstore on-site. Rangers present programs throughout the day.

Tour the East or West Rim scenic drives. (See Overlooks for information and highlights of each.) You can leave the park by the East Rim Drive; the West Rim Drive deadends at Hermits Rest.

See Tusayan Museum and Ruin near the park's east entrance, a forty-five minute drive one way from Grand Canyon Village. A self-guiding trail explores the site and nearby agricultural fields of ancestral Pueblo people who abandoned this settlement 800 years ago. Ranger-led programs are also scheduled. Check *THE GUIDE* for times. There are exhibits of artifacts in the museum, and a bookstore.

Take a walk on the Rim Trail (See Rim Walking Trails). Brochures on natural and human history are available from trailside dispenser boxes or at NPS visitor information centers. Grand Canyon Association bookstores have low-cost informational brochures and checklists as well as more comprehensive books pertaining to all aspects of the Canyon.

Explore the Historic District (See Park Buildings & Landmarks).

Hit the trail (See Day Hikes into the Canyon) to get that inner-canyon feeling. Even a short hike below the rim will be worthwhile. Grand Canyon Association bookstores have numerous inexpensive brochures and maps for specific trails.

Watch the sunrise or sunset. Check *THE GUIDE* for times. Any area from which you have broad views of the Canyon is good; note on the map points that extend far out into the Canyon. The rim area near the lodges, Yavapai and Lipan Points, and Desert View are all outstanding and have easy automobile access and parking. Don't forget that the West Rim Drive is closed to private automobiles in the summer (See Getting Around in the Park, Free In-Park Shuttle Bus). Dress warmly for sunrise.

Watch the mule trips depart for Phantom Ranch from the corral near the West Rim Interchange. Departure times change with the season; check with the Bright Angel Transportation Desk for current information.

Viewing sunrise or sunset at Grand Canyon can be an inspirational experience.
Photo by George H. H. Huey

Take a commercial tour (See Commercial Tours, South Rim).

ACTIVITIES

WINTER

Cross-country skiing and snowshoeing—Can be enjoyed almost anywhere in the forest. The USFS sometimes grooms trails near Grandview Point. For your safety, please stay back from the rim. Equipment can be rented from Babbitt's General Store. See Grand Canyon Village, Other Facilities and Services.

Snowmobiles may not be used anywhere within the park.

Birdwatching

Christmas Bird Count—Check with park personnel at any NPS information center for details.

Meteor showers—Quantratids in January

SPRING

Cactus bloom—Inner canyon beginning in April

Birdwatching

Meteors showers—Eta Aquarids late April–May

SUMMER

Wildflowers on the rim

Birdwatching

Meteor showers—Perseids second week in August

FALL

Raptor migration—September–October

Birdwatching

Wildflowers on the rim

Meteor showers—Orionids late October, Andromedids and Leonids in November; Geminids in December

■ RIM WALKING TRAILS

The Rim Trail is paved from Yavapai Point west to Maricopa Point, about three miles, and continues, unpaved, from Maricopa to Hermits Rest and the Hermit trailhead, an additional six miles. The views are non-stop and breathtaking. Few Grand Canyon trails or walks are "level" in the city sense, and the Rim Trail has its ups and downs. Persons using wheelchairs can travel most of the paved section from Yavapai Point west to Kolb Studio, with some assistance for there are some steep stretches. From Kolb Studio west, not only is it steep in places but there are steps. The trail can be icy and snowpacked during winter (See Grand Canyon Village map).

NPS Visitor Center to the Rim: A ½-mile, level, paved trail continues past Mather Amphitheater, the site of park service evening programs, to connect with the Rim Trail.

The Visitor Center has water and restrooms. There are chemical toilets and water at Yavapai Point and Hermits Rest, near the Hopi House parking lot, in the parking lot just west of Bright Angel Lodge, and near the West Rim Interchange. There is a chemical toilet at Hopi Point during the summer only.

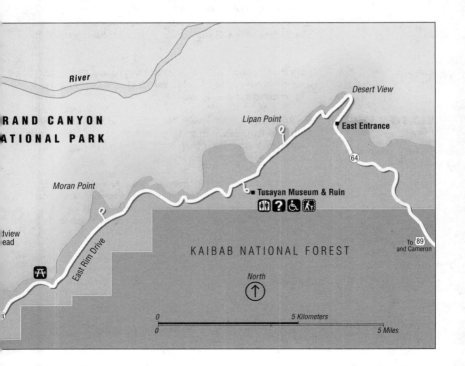

■ Day Hikes into the Canyon

Day hikers on the South Kaibab Trail.

Getting below the rim gives an entirely different canyon experience. There are several trails that provide ideal day-hiking opportunities. Prepare as carefully for a day hike as you would for an overnighter; the conditions are the same. Refer to the Safety section for information on how to prepare for your hike, and prevention and treatment of hiking-related illness. Hiking permits are required only for overnight hiking trips.

Trails from the South Rim can be icy and snowpacked during winter. Instep crampons may be advisable. Babbitt's General Store rents and sells crampons and other equipment.

WORDS OF WISDOM

The Bright Angel, South Kaibab, North Kaibab, Hermit, and Tanner Trails go to the Colorado River. Do not be tempted to hike from rim to river and back in one day. Many people who try collapse; some die. If you become exhausted and try to spend the night without an overnight camping permit, you will be fined and required to hike out anyway, no matter how tired you feel. Unless you are experiencing a life-threatening illness or injury, the only way out is on your own two feet. Helicopters and other evacuation measures are used only for dire medical emergencies (and at the hiker's expense), and no amount of money will hire you one otherwise.

Everyone hikes at their own speed. Do not leave a slower hiker alone and do not push people to hike faster than is comfortable for them. Day hikers account for 60 percent of the search and rescue efforts conducted on Grand Canyon trails. Canyon hiking is some of the world's most demanding and must be approached with common sense.

On *any* canyon hike, carry water and food and use it.

THE WELL-EQUIPPED DAY HIKER

I've seen people headed down the Bright Angel Trail in high-heeled sandals; others carrying ice chests; men and women in tiny little bathing suits, packs chaffing away on their backs. My brother gave me a terrible jolt by saying he believed he would hike in his cowboy boots. Without going too far in the conservative direction, consider outfitting yourself with at least the following:

Comfortable shoes—For most people heavy-duty hiking boots are not necessary on the Bright Angel or Kaibab Trails. Unless you have problem feet or ankles, you will probably do very well with comfortable, well broken-in walking shoes with enough tread to provide good traction. For Hermit, Grandview and other unmaintained trails, hiking boots are recommended.

Hat and shirt—In warm weather it is very important to keep the sun off your head and upper body. If you become overheated, you can pour water on your hat and shirt to help cool down.

Water—Grand Canyon's air is extremely dry, and your body will lose more moisture than you realize. Carry water on any walk or hike. In warm weather, carry one gallon per person per day. And *drink* it.

Snacks—Take along nutritious and high-energy foods; candy, nuts, fruit, cheese. And *eat* it.

Layered clothing—In cooler months and even late on a summer day, wear a wind- and water-resistant outer garment. Layered clothing can be removed or added as needed to maintain a safe body temperature.

First-aid kit—With moleskin for blisters and "hot spots."

Maps—Grand Canyon Association bookstores in park visitor contact stations sell hiking guides for major trails and a variety of maps.

Pack—Comfortable and well adjusted.

Flashlight—In case you don't get to the rim before dark.

BRIGHT ANGEL TRAILHEAD TO INDIAN GARDEN & PLATEAU POINT

Round-trip hiking distance:
 Indian Garden—9 miles
 Indian Garden to Plateau Point—3 miles
Vertical descent: 3,000 feet
Round-trip hiking time: 7 hours. Add 2 hours for Plateau Point.
Water at Mile-and-a-Half and Three-Mile Resthouses (May through September only), and Indian Garden
Pit toilets at Mile-and-a-Half Resthouse and Indian Garden. Picnic tables and shade at Indian Garden. No facilities at Plateau Point

The trailhead is just west of Kolb Studio in the Historic District, with easy access by automobile or shuttle bus. Park in the lots near the Bright Angel Lodge.

AY HIKES INTO THE CANYON

The Bright Angel Trail, well developed, well marked, and well maintained, is the most used Canyon trail, so don't expect solitude. The trail continues to the Colorado River and Phantom Ranch. It is not recommended that anyone hike from the rim to the river and back in one day.

The Bright Angel is the route into the Canyon for the passenger mules and they have the right-of-way on the trail. When you encounter them, for your safety, stand quietly to the inside of the trail and follow any instructions given by the wrangler. Mules will be mules, and they create a lot of residue; watch your step.

SOUTH KAIBAB TRAILHEAD TO CEDAR RIDGE

Round-trip hiking distance: 3 miles
Vertical descent: 1,500 feet
Round-trip hiking time: 3 hours
Pit toilet at Cedar Ridge
Water available during warm months

The trailhead is at Yaki Point, one mile east of the South Rim Entrance Road/East Rim Drive junction From mid-March through mid-October, the park provides free shuttle bus service to Yaki Point, and no private vehicles are allowed at Yaki Point during that period of time. Check *THE GUIDE* for current schedules.

The South Kaibab Trail, well developed, well marked, and well maintained, continues to the Colorado River and Phantom Ranch. Going all the way to the river and back in one day is strongly discouraged.

The South Kaibab is the route out of the Canyon for the passenger mules, and both in and out for supply mules, and they have the right-of-way on trails. When you encounter mules, for your safety, stand quietly to the inside of the trail and follow any instructions given by the wrangler.

GRANDVIEW TRAILHEAD TO HORSESHOE MESA

Round-trip hiking distance: 6 miles
Vertical descent: 2,600 feet
Round-trip hiking time: 7 hours
No water available
Pit toilet at Horseshoe Mesa

The trailhead is at the parking area at Grandview Point, about eleven miles east of the South Rim Entrance Road/East Rim Drive junction, with easy access by automobile.

The Grandview is a wilderness trail. It is not regularly maintained and there will be some washouts and boulders strewn on the trail. Here you will find solitude and indescribable views. Everyone who hikes the Canyon has their obnoxious tales, but, the first time I approached Grandview Trail, I just could not do it. Acrophobia reigned supreme. After acclimating on other trails, I succeeded in clamoring down to Horseshoe Mesa (and back) on numerous occasions. The point is, there are some steep and tight switchbacks on this narrow trail. Keep in mind there is no shame in occasionally lowering your center of gravity by sitting down and scooting along on your bottom.

Warning: Do not enter mineshafts; there are high levels of radon gas and numerous other hazards.

HERMIT TRAILHEAD TO SANTA MARIA SPRINGS

Round-trip hiking distance: 5 miles
Vertical descent: 2,160 feet
Round-trip hiking time: 7 hours
No water or toilet facilities

Trailhead is at the end of the service road behind Hermits Rest, located at the end of West Rim Drive, eight miles west of Grand Canyon Village. The West Rim Drive is closed to private vehicles during the summer, usually from mid-March through mid-October. During that time a free shuttle bus runs to Hermits Rest. Check the bus schedule in *THE GUIDE*, available free at the NPS Visitor Center and other locations throughout the park. There is no free shuttle bus to Hermits Rest at any other time.

The Hermit Trail is a wilderness trail, not regularly maintained. You may encounter trail washouts and have to use some route-finding skills.

■ OVERLOOKS

Along the thirty miles of South Rim road are numerous overlooks. Each is spectacular and provides its unique perspective on the Canyon, and it would not be redundant to stop at more than one or even all of them. Most points have excellent interpretive panels that explain pertinent human or natural history. There are parking lots at all. Those that have restrooms, water, or are wheelchair accessible are designated. * The West Rim Drive and Yaki Point are closed to most private vehicle traffic from mid-March through mid-October, during which time a free shuttle bus is provided (See Getting Around in the Park, Free In-Park Shuttle Bus).

Windshield views are possible from Navajo and Lipan Points and from many pull-outs along the East and West Rim drives.

Many features are visible from more than one point: To the east, the scalloped Palisades of the Desert (seventeen miles away), Navajo Mountain (ninety miles distant) on a clear day, and the Echo and Vermilion Cliffs (forty to fifty miles). To the north, Marble Platform and the Kaibab Plateau (ten miles). To the south, the San Francisco Peaks (sixty miles), Red Butte (seventeen miles). To the west, Mt. Trumbull (fifty-seven miles).

	Restrooms	Water	Windshield Views	Trailhead	Accessible Path	Exhibit
Desert View	♿				■	■
Navajo Point			■			
Lipan Point			■	Tanner		■
Moran Point					■	■
Grandview Point				Grandview		■
Yaki Point*	chemical; at trailhead	seasonal		S. Kaibab		■
Mather Point					■	■
Yavapai Point	♿ chemical	■				■
Trailview I & II*						■
Maricopa Point*						
Powell Point*						■
Hopi Point*	chemical; summer only					■
Mohave Point*						■
The Abyss*			■			■
Pima Point*						■
Hermits Rest*	■	■		Hermit	■	■

The Colorado River is visible from the rim at Desert View, Navajo, Lipan, Moran, Mather, Yavapai, Hopi, Mohave, and Pima Points. Distance from rim viewing points makes the river seem but a creek; however, it averages three hundred feet in width.

Mather Point is probably the most-visited overlook on the South Rim.

PS Info Center	Gift Shop	Snack Bar	Phone	Ranger Programs	Bookstore	Highlights
■	■	■	■		■	Watchtower
						Views of Unkar Delta, Hance & Unkar Rapids, raptor migration Sept–Oct
						View of Horseshoe Mesa
		■				Views of inner canyon trails
						By far the most visited point on either rim
■				■	■	Provides indoor panoramic views
						Views of trails and distant landmarks
						Orphan Mine visible
						Orphan Mine visible
						Granite Rapid visible
						Hermit, Granite, Salt Creek Rapids visible
						Great Mohave Wall drops 3,000 feet to Tonto Platform; good birding
						Good western canyon views
		summer				Historic building; snack bar (seasonally)

■ COMMERCIAL TOURS

Grand Canyon National Park Lodges ☎, a Grand Canyon National Park concessioner offers a variety of tours throughout the year. Prices given are ranges only and are subject to change. They should be viewed as guidelines only.

If you are already in the park, tours may be purchased at any Grand Canyon National Park Lodge transportation desk (listed below). Coach tours include East and West Rim; Wupatki, Sunset Crater Volcano, and Walnut Canyon National Monuments; Monument Valley expedition (coach only or coach/air combination); smooth water river raft excursion; coach/train combinations to and from Williams, Arizona, with Grand Canyon Railway. Tours last from two to thirteen hours, and adult fares for ground tours range from $11 to $80, and around $230 for ground/air tours.

Mule trips have been offered at Grand Canyon for almost one hundred years. In fact, they were the reason Phantom Ranch was built in 1922. (They are mules, not donkeys, by the way.) Riders must weigh less than two hundred pounds fully dressed, including equipment, be at least 4' 7" in height, fluent in English, and not pregnant. One-day trips to Plateau Point, and two- and three-day trips with overnight stay at Phantom Ranch are offered. Prices range from $100 for the day trip to about $350 per person (including all meals and accommodations) for overnighters. Overnight trips offer substantial discounts for parties of more than one person. Make reservations as far in advance as possible by calling or writing AMFAC Parks & Resorts ☎. If you are in the park and do not have reservations, check at the Bright Angel Transportation Desk around 7 A.M. for cancellations.

Mule riders on the Bright Angel Trail just below Kolb Studio.

Grand Canyon National Park Lodges Transportation Desks provide information on and sell mule, coach and air tours; horseback rides; taxis.

Bright Angel Lodge Transportation Desk handles check-in for Phantom Ranch lodging and meals, and mule trips. Open daily year round 6 A.M.–7 P.M.

Maswik Lodge Transportation Desk open daily year round 10 A.M. to 4 P.M. Hours may vary seasonally.

Yavapai Lodge Transportation Desk open seasonally, usually from April through October, 9 A.M.–5 P.M.

Grand Canyon National Park Lodges staffs a desk in the National Park Service Visitor Center from April through October. Hours are 10 A.M.–4 P.M. but may vary.

Daily excursion trains operate from Williams to Grand Canyon.

Grand Canyon Railway ☎, a Grand Canyon National Park concessioner, runs excursion trains from Williams, Arizona, to the Canyon daily, except December 24 and 25. Three classes of service are offered with adult fares ranging from $49 to $99 per person, children from $19 to $69. Trains depart Williams at 9:30 A.M., arrive at Grand Canyon at 11:45 A.M.; depart Grand Canyon at 3:15 P.M. Overnight packages and optional return by bus are also available. Canyon rim tours by Grand Canyon National Park Lodges coaches have been arranged to accommodate the train schedule, and plane/train packages with Scenic Airlines are available. Prices are subject to change. Write or call for brochures and full information.

Air tours in fixed-wing aircraft and helicopters originate outside the park. Numerous local air-tour operators are located at Grand Canyon Airport. To obtain a list of commercial air tour operators write Grand Canyon Chamber of Commerce ☎.

River trips through Grand Canyon, from three days' to three weeks' duration, are available. Photo by George H. H. Huey

White water rafting companies (See Addresses and Telephone Numbers, White Water Rafting Companies) ☎ are Grand Canyon National Park concessioners. Trips through Grand Canyon on the Colorado River, three days to three weeks in duration, require reservations well in advance. Oar-powered and paddle rafts, kayaks, and motorized craft are used. Generally, prices (not including other transportation) will range from about $150 per day up. Contact the operators directly for specific information.

■ Park Buildings & Landmarks

SHRINE OF THE AGES, just west of the NPS Visitor Center, was built with private donations in 1967 as a worship site for all faiths. Ownership of the building was transferred to the National Park Service in 1975, and it is now made available for visitor and community programs and events.

GRAND CANYON CEMETERY is located just west of the Shrine of the Ages. The cemetery's 304 plots are reserved for people who have worked in the park and their immediate families. Exceptions may be made for persons who have contributed significantly to the park or to public understanding and appreciation of its resources. Headstones bear the names of prospectors, early settlers, Harvey Girls, wranglers, trail guides, artists, and government officials, among them John Hance, W.W. Bass, Pete Berry, Ralph Cameron, the Kolb brothers, John Verkamp, and Gunnar Widforss. There is a memorial to the 128 passengers killed in 1956 when United and TWA airliners collided 20,000 feet above the Canyon.

Daniel L. Hogan, a New York native living in Flagstaff, came to the Canyon in 1890 to prospect and within several months found copper ore about 1,000 feet below Maricopa Point. He filed the **ORPHAN MINE** claim, including a small amount of rim acreage, in 1893. Because of the difficulty of bringing ore out of the Canyon and the expense of transporting it to El Paso, Texas, for processing, this mine, like others in the Canyon, was not profitable and much of the time was not active. Hogan pursued a small construction business in Flagstaff and returned to the mine when things were slow. He and Buckey O'Neill, another canyon miner and entrepreneur, joined Teddy Roosevelt's Rough Riders in Cuba during the Spanish-American War in 1898. O'Neill was killed there but Hogan returned to his enterprises. He retained his small in-holding after the park was established in 1919 though the federal government wanted the land. In the 1930s he built a number of tourist cabins and a trading post on the rim portion of his claim, but it suffered when World War II squelched travel. In 1947 he sold his claim to Mrs. Madeline Jacobs of Prescott, Arizona, who envisioned using the site for a lodge. Ore assays revealed rich uranium content and after the forest service blocked her hotel development plan for a number of years, Mrs. Jacobs sold the mineral and surface rights and the existing tourist buildings to the Golden Crown Mining Company. During the 1950s the mine and its ore boosted northern Arizona's economy but by 1960 was playing out. The government and the mining company came to an agreement in 1962 allowing the mining of uranium under national park land until 1987, when the land would become park property. The mine suspended operations in 1966. Dan Hogan died in 1957 at the age of ninety, having developed and retired from a prosperous building construction business in Flagstaff. The buildings have been removed from the site, leaving only the headframe standing.

The headframe of the Orphan Mine is visible from many points along the South Rim.

Fred Harvey Company opened **HOPI HOUSE**, one of the first curio shops at Grand Canyon, about the same time as El Tovar in 1905. Mary Colter, who had started designing architecture for Fred Harvey three years earlier, sought to create buildings that reflected local culture. Hopi House, Colter's first design for Grand Canyon Village,

was inspired by the Hopi pueblo Oraibi, the oldest continually inhabited village in the United States. Hopi Indians did much of the construction work using local stone and wood. Hopi artists lived in the building

Hopi House was one of the first curio shops at Grand Canyon.

and visitors could watch them as they wove blankets, and made pottery, jewelry, and baskets for sale. Hopi House is on the National Register of Historic Places.

The Santa Fe Railway Company brought its first train to the Canyon in 1901 and immediately began plans for a first-class hotel. **EL TOVAR** was designed by Charles Whittlesey in the manner of a European alpine lodge. The one-hundred-room hotel was completed in 1905 at a cost of $250,000 and was described as "the most expensively constructed and appointed log house in America." The four-story structure was made of native stone and Douglas-fir logs brought in by train from Oregon. It had steam heat, electric lights, and one bath on each floor. For the comfort and enjoyment of guests it provided art and music rooms, ladies' lounging room, club room, solarium, grotto,

and roof gardens. It also had its own power plant and laundry. The Fred Harvey Company ran all of the hotels and restaurants along the Santa Fe's lines, and El Tovar's kitchen, like those at other Harvey establishments, had bakery and butcher shops, and bulk storage refrigerators for the fine produce and meat which were brought in from across the country. The Fred Harvey dairy at Del Rio, 120 miles south of the Canyon, provided fresh milk. Harvey Girls, in black dresses with white aprons, served. El Tovar is on the National Register of Historic Places.

El Tovar, opened in 1905, was designed in the manner of a European alpine lodge.

YAVAPAI OBSERVATION STATION is a "trailside museum," intended to give the visitor information in a conveniently located structure, and was designed to highlight the geology of Grand Canyon. It was built in 1927–1928 with funds from the Laura Spelman Rockefeller Foundation. Its designer, Herbert Maier, also designed museums at Yellowstone and Yosemite National Parks during the same period. He believed that "exhibit rooms should afford an occasional vista into the nearby woodland so that the visitor may have a feeling of being in the midst of the subject matter that is being interpreted." Maier's designs honored the spirit of the surrounding culture and landscape, and in this regard Yavapai reflects the influence of Mary Colter's architecture. Maier selected stone quarried from the Canyon and supervised the positioning of each stone during construction. The building's flat roof, small window openings, and vigas are distinctly pueblo design traits. It has undergone interior renovations, but its Canyon focus remains primary.

PARK BUILDINGS & LANDMARKS

John Verkamp came to the Canyon at the turn of the century to sell curios for Babbitt Brothers' Trading Company from a tent on the canyon rim. He built his own store in 1905, a two-story building combining Pueblo and Mission Revival styles. The Verkamp family still own and operate **VERKAMPS CURIOS**. A large painting by Louis Akin, muralist for Southwest Indian Room of the American Museum of Natural History, is displayed on the shop's main floor. Before any of them moved to Arizona, the Verkamp and Babbitt families had been acquainted in Cincinnati, Ohio. Three Babbitt brothers married Verkamp sisters, in fact. Both families became highly regarded in the state, and remain active in politics as well as business.

Lookout Studio seems very much a part of the Canyon rim.

The Fred Harvey Company built the Lookout (now known as **LOOKOUT STUDIO**) in 1914. Mary Colter designed and decorated the building, which sold photographic prints, books about the Canyon, and provided telescopes for canyon viewing. The building's design was inspired by Hopi Indian structures, and with its low, uneven lines, weeds growing between the roof stones, and a chimney that appeared to be piled-up rocks, it looked like part of the canyon rim.

In 1896 J. Wilbur Thurber, who ran a stage line from Flagstaff, started the Bright Angel Hotel near the rim, around which grew up a motley collection of buildings and tents called Bright Angel Camp. The train put the stage line out of business, and the Santa Fe Railway bought the hotel in 1901. The railway replaced the buildings of Bright Angel Camp and Bright Angel Hotel in 1935 with **BRIGHT ANGEL LODGE**, designed and decorated by Mary Colter. Built at a total cost of $500,000 it included shops, restaurants, and an array of cabins. Two historic cabins were incorporated by Colter: Red Horse Station, which had served as a rest stop on the stagecoach line and later as Grand Canyon Village's first post office; and the cabin of Buckey O'Neill. Built of native materials, the lodge's lobby featured rough wooden walls, a log ceiling, and flagstone floors. Above the recessed fireplace in the lobby Colter placed a wooden thunderbird, long the symbol of the Fred Harvey Indian Detours. In the lounge Colter built a "geologic fireplace," ten feet high, recreating the rock layers of the Canyon. Stone from each canyon layer was selected by park naturalists and carried out by mule. Two thousand people attended the opening barbecue, Hopi Indians danced and cowboys sang.

Originally **RED HORSE STATION** had served stagecoaches south of Grandview Point. Ralph Cameron moved it to the canyon rim about 1902 and added a porch and second story to make the Cameron Hotel. From 1910 to 1935 it served as the United States Post Office. Mary Colter restored the rough-hewn square log cabin and incorporated it into the Bright Angel Lodge in 1935.

Buckey O'Neill, an early canyon settler with a background in law, writing, education, business, and mineral prospecting, built his cabin

on the rim in 1896 or 1897. O'Neill was part owner ~
Mines fifteen miles south of the Canyon and had persu~
company to build a railroad line from ~ ~s to
Anita to carry out ore. When the mines played out,
the Santa Fe Railway bought the line and extended it
to the rim. O'Neill sold his cabin to the Santa Fe
when they bought Thurber's Bright Angel Hotel and
Camp. Mary Colter incorporated it into the Bright
Angel Lodge as part of a larger structure. O'Neill
was with Teddy Roosevelt's Rough Riders in Cuba,
and was killed the day before the charge up San Juan
Hill. **BUCKEY O'NEILL CABIN** is on the National
Register of Historic Places.

The Buckey O'Neill Cabin.

COLTER HALL, the Fred Harvey Company's women's dormitory,
was built just south of El Tovar in 1937. It is named for its architect
and is still used as employee housing by Grand Canyon National Park
Lodges. Numerous duplex
and single-family houses and
men's dormitories, Victor
Hall and Victor Annex, built
by the Santa Fe in the 1920s,
are still used as residences.

**THE MULE BARN,
LIVERY STABLE** (with
cupola), and **BLACKSMITH
SHOP** were built by the
Santa Fe Railway in 1907.
They provided mules, horses,
carriages, and stages used
for the Fred Harvey
Company's early-day tours.
Today they are used for the

The historic Mule Barn and
stables continue to house
mules that carry passengers and supplies into the Canyon. Honest-to-
gers and supplies into the goodness wranglers and blacksmiths are in attendance. All three
canyon. buildings are on the National Register of Historic Places.

GRAND CANYON DEPOT was built by the Santa Fe Railway in
1909, and is one of three remaining log depots of the fourteen known
to have been built in the United States. Architect Francis Wilson had
designed the home of the Santa Fe's president as well as depots and
hotels along Santa Fe's lines. He planned the depot, his only rustic or
log building, as a counterpart to El Tovar. The first story included a
waiting room, ticket office, baggage room, restrooms, and offices. Its
floor was of scored concrete. The second story was an apartment for
the station manager. In 1968 Santa Fe passenger service terminated.
After the building became park service property in 1982 it was used
variously as offices, interpretive center, and concession space. The
new Grand Canyon Railway refurbished the building in 1989. Park
service offices currently occupy the second floor. The depot is on the
National Register of Historic Places.

THE POWER HOUSE was built in 1926 by the Santa Fe Railway to provide power and steam heat for its rim facilities and steam heat for railway cars parked in the railyard. Because of its ingenious design, is perhaps the most interesting structure at Grand Canyon. Unfortunately the architect remains unknown. Its chalet style, compatible with the depot and El Tovar, is used in this instance at almost twice the usual size. The upper windows are seven feet high; the balcony railing, five feet high; the eave overhang, five feet. Even stones used on the exterior are oversized. Consequently, viewers note the familiar design elements and perceive the building to be half the size it actually is. Two Fairbanks-Morse diesel generators remain in the building with their original labels: Indian Garden pump; El Tovar; fire pump; Bright Angel lights and power; USNPS; train yard, turbine cooling tower; power house. The Santa Fe sold the building to the park service in 1954 and power operations ceased in 1956. It is now used as storage space and offices for the park concessioner. It is on the National Register of Historic Places.

KOLB STUDIO evolved over more than twenty years' time. Ellsworth Kolb came to the Canyon from Pennsylvania in 1901 and his brother Emery followed a year later. They purchased a photographic studio in Williams, Arizona, with plans to move it to the canyon rim. Strained relations with the federal government began early on when they were denied permission by the United States Forester, under pressure from the Fred Harvey Company, to open a studio at the Canyon. By 1903 the Kolbs had persuaded Ralph Cameron to let them pitch a tent studio on his rim property; they used an old mining site below the rim for a darkroom. In 1904 Cameron let them build a small wooden structure from which they photographed mule riders as they began

Kolb Studio began as a small structure in 1904 and evolved over the next twenty years into its present four levels that spill over the Canyon rim.

their day trips down the Bright Angel Trail. The new studio lacked water, however, and to develop their glass photographic plates the brothers built a darkroom $4^1/2$ miles below the rim at Indian Garden. Every day until about 1930, when water finally became available on the rim, Emery ran past the mule riders as he began the 3,000-foot vertical descent, developed the plates, and returned to the rim in time to sell photographs to the riders as they returned at the end of the day. By 1911 the adventuresome brothers had decided to duplicate John Wesley Powell's 1869 Colorado River exploration. Since Powell, only a handful of people had run the river (and as few as one hundred as late as the 1950s). The Kolbs not only succeeded in completing the trip, 101 days long, they captured it on motion picture film. They showed the film in Ohio, an unprofitable venture because Ellsworth took the booking without a guaranteed fee, which spawned a bitter feud between the two men. Subsequent showings in the eastern United States contributed largely to public awareness of Grand Canyon. Ellsworth moved from the Canyon after the disagreement and lived in California until his death in 1960. Emery expanded the studio in 1915 and once more in 1925. He did much of the work and it is obvious that little professional planning or design were sought. The structure eventually grew into four levels spilling over the canyon rim,

and included an auditorium, a gift shop, telescope r
and living quarters for Emery, his wife, and daughte
picture of the river trip was shown every day in the studio auditorium,
personally narrated by Emery. He lived in the building until his death
in 1976 at ninety-five, at which time ownership transferred to the
National Park Service. Both Emery and Ellsworth are buried in the
Grand Canyon Cemetery. The park service was unable to devote the
amount of money needed to renovate the structure and it sat empty
and unused until 1990. The Grand Canyon Association was permitted
by the park to open a bookstore on the first floor and devoted Kolb
Studio bookstore earnings to the renovation, rehabilitation and ongoing upkeep of the building. The auditorium now is an exhibit hall,
and administrative use is made of the lower levels.

The Santa Fe Railway constructed an
eight-mile road for touring stages along
the rim west of Grand Canyon Village in
1912, and at its end built a rest stop for
passengers. **HERMITS REST**, designed
by Mary Colter, was completed in 1914
at a cost of $13,000. Colter designed the
new rest stop to have the character of a
retreat built with gathered materials,
something a hermit might assemble.
She covered the fireplace stones with soot to attest to long years of
service. For the entry gate she fashioned an arch of stones, seemingly
casually stacked, and a broken bell she found in New Mexico. As Fred
Harvey passengers refreshed themselves at Hermits Rest, they were
served free tea and wafers; others paid fifty cents. The site was named
for Louis Boucher, the "hermit" who lived below the rim at Dripping
Springs from 1889 until about 1909. Boucher, a Canadian, was one of
the first European-Americans to arrive at the Canyon. He built a trail

**The fanciful Hermits Rest
was designed by Mary
Colter to look like a retreat
a hermit might have built.**

(Dripping Springs Trail) from the rim to his camp at Dripping Springs
and later another trail (Boucher Trail) to his copper mine. He was not
a hermit, as he was labeled in later years, but welcomed guests to his
inner-canyon homesites and worked with Pete Berry and John Hance
as a tourist guide. In 1909 he sold his trails and holdings to the Santa
Fe Railway. Between 1911 and 1914 the company improved the upper
portions of Boucher's trail and extended it to their newly built Hermit
Creek Camp. It is the only canyon trail built especially for tourists.
The camp, 3,500 feet and 7$^{1}/_{2}$ miles by trail below the rim, included
sleeping cabins with electricity and telephone service. After 1925 an
aerial tramway from Pima Point provided access. National Park
Service restrictions on inner canyon use required that the camp and
tramway be removed, which was accomplished by 1936.

When Americans began to travel again after World War I the Fred
Harvey Company and the Santa Fe Railway decided to build lodging
for their mule riders at the bottom of the Canyon. Mary Colter
designed the retreat, which she named **PHANTOM RANCH**. It was
completed in 1922, and featured "a large combined dining room and
restroom, three large cabins with wide sleeping porches for the
accommodation of visitors and a caretaker's cabin. . . . The cabins
have all the comforts of home—shower baths, running water and

. BUILDINGS & LANDMARKS

telephones." The Craftsman Bungalow cabins were built of stone gathered on location, but all other materials had to be brought in by mule. The cabins were sparsely furnished—two beds, desk, and chair—but also included a fireplace and an Indian rug on the floor.

Aiming for the resort to be self-sufficient, orchards of peach, plum, and apricot trees were planted. A chicken house and black-smith shop were later covered by a land-slide. The Civilian Conservation Corps built a swimming pool in 1934. Though the pool was enormously popular, by the 1960s, given increased use of Phantom Ranch, it became a maintenance and health problem and was filled in. Today the ranch is much different, with added buildings and alterations to the originals, but its rustic romanticism has not been lost.

The rustic romanticism of Phantom Ranch exists today much as it did in the twenties.

The **WATCHTOWER** was designed by the Harvey Company's architect Mary Colter to serve as a gift shop and resting place for the company's sightseeing tours. Desert View offered a dramatic panoramic view, and Colter intended to make the most of it. With customary attention to detail and authenticity, for six months she visited, photographed, and sketched prehistoric tower remains throughout the Southwest. It was not her intention to replicate them, but to use their features to give cultural richness to her building. She built a model of the site, complete with existing plants and shrubs, and placed on it a model of the tower. Having determined that the building suited the location, she had a seventy-foot-high wooden scaffolding built on the location so she could evaluate the views of the Canyon and the San Francisco Peaks from this vantage point. The steel framework for the tower was fabricated by the Santa Fe Railway and set on a concrete foundation. Stone for the structure was gathered locally. Huge windows provided canyon views from the entry room, which had rustic furniture made of tree trunks and wood burls. Stairs led up to the Hopi Room which Colter hired Hopi Indian artist Fred Kabotie to paint. Kabotie, who would later gain international fame, used a Hopi Indian snake dance motif. By sprinkling pinches of colored sand, he made an intricate sand painting in the ancestral manner. After the building's dedication, the sand painting was not destroyed as traditional ceremonial use would have required, but small alterations were made and it was preserved under glass. A stairway, curved along the interior walls of the tower, led to the upper galleries, which were painted by Fred Greer. The archaeological sites at Abo, New Mexico, from which they were copied, have since been destroyed. Greer's paintings may be the only existing records. The Watchtower's dedication ceremony in 1933 included American Indian dances and blessings, and was covered by radio broadcast, film, and 620 newspapers.

TUSAYAN RUIN is the site of an 800-year-old ancestral Pueblo dwelling. The small U-shaped pueblo has eight habitation rooms enclosing a small plaza. There are two kivas, and a few hundred yards away are agricultural plots with check dams. The settlement site was

The excavated Tusayan Ruin is a glimpse at life at Grand Canyon 800 years ago.

first noted during an archaeological survey in 1923. During its excavation in 1930, archaeologists left one row of storage rooms in tact to facilitate interpretation. Tree-ring dating from Tusayan Ruin yielded the first absolute archaeological dates for the South Rim. Artifacts recovered were put on permanent display in the museum, which was built with funds donated by Mrs. Winifred MacCurdy of Pasadena, California.

DRINKING WATER— WHERE DOES IT COME FROM?

The upper 3,000 feet of canyon rock layers are porous, highly fractured limestone; rainfall and snowmelt soak right through them, leaving no standing surface water on either rim.

For many years, railroad tank cars hauled water from 120 miles away for South Rim use. Even after a pipeline was brought from Garden Creek, demand soon exceeded supply.

The park service began construction in 1960 on a cross-canyon pipeline. Water would enter the line at Roaring Springs, 3,000 feet below the North Rim where groundwater reaches an impermeable rock layer and rushes out. It would be carried by gravity flow down canyon walls and across the river to Indian Garden and pumped from there to the South Rim for storage. Installation of twelve miles of pipeline in canyon topography was a task of heroic proportions. Helicopters brought in workers, machinery, and materials. Pipe was buried where possible; laid on top of the ground or pinned to canyon walls in many places.

In early December 1966, as work was almost completed, a fourteen-inch rainfall brought flashfloods that all but destroyed the line. With renewed funding and effort, it was completed in 1970 and still serves the South Rim's needs. Occasional rockfalls or corroded pipes interrupt service and conservation measures over and above the usual judicious water use are called for.

North Rim water is brought from Roaring Springs by a powerhouse and pumping station built by the Union Pacific Railroad in 1928.

■ THE INNER CANYON

Extending up from the Colorado River to the rims of the Canyon is the segment of the park that is known as the inner canyon. Most of it is inaccessible, and what can be reached is gained by foot or mule only. Today sixteen hiking trails and numerous recognized routes enter the Canyon, most developed from prehistoric Indian routes, which in turn were probably developed from animal trails. Not surprisingly then, the trails lead ultimately to water—seeps, springs, creeks, the river.

The most heavily used trails are the Bright Angel and North and South Kaibab Trails, designated as Corridor Trails. All three converge at Phantom Ranch, near the Colorado River. There Grand Canyon National Park Lodges operates the only lodging and meal service within the inner canyon.

The Bright Angel and South and North Kaibab Trails all provide excellent day hiking (See Day Hikes into the Canyon). Although these trails go to the river, hiking rim-to-river and back in one day is strongly discouraged. To plan overnight hikes see Overnight Hiking, Backcountry Permits for information on the requirements for permits and reservations.

From the South Rim you can see the Tonto Trail running east/west along the Tonto Platform. This ninety-two-mile-long trail is seldom hiked in its entirety, but is used to connect rim-to-river trails. Although it appears to be level, it isn't; it veers wildly as it crosses steep and deep drainages.

The broad Tonto Platform, 3,000 feet below the rim, is a dramatic desert environment. Photo by George H. H. Huey

Indian Garden is conspicuous as the greenest area on the Tonto Platform. It is a popular day- or overnight-hiking destination with picnic tables, campground, ranger station, drinking water, and pit toilets (See Day Hikes into the Canyon, Bright Angel Trail). (Hiking permits are required for all overnight hikes. See Backcountry Permits & Overnight Hiking.) Garden Creek flows year round, and cottonwood trees shade its banks.

The long straight trail continuing north from Indian Garden leads to Plateau Point, an overlook of the Inner Gorge and the Colorado River.

Seen from the rim, the broad Tonto Platform, 3,000 feet below, may seem to be the bottom of the Canyon, but below it the Inner Gorge, a gorge within a gorge, plunges another 1,500 vertical feet. The Bright Angel Trail continues down the break just northeast of Indian Garden.

There are two footbridges crossing the Colorado River and both are in close proximity to Phantom Ranch. The Kaibab Suspension Bridge, sometimes called the black bridge, built in 1928, is 440 feet long

THE INNER CANYON

and 78 feet above the river's low-water level. The eight steel cables required for its construction, weighing a total of 19,000 pounds, were carried into the Canyon by a procession of forty-two Havasupai Indian men. The carriers spaced themselves out, hoisted the cable onto their shoulders to distribute the weight to about fifty-five pounds per man, and inched down the South Kaibab Trail. Each of the eight round-trips required two days.

About two miles downstream from the Kaibab Suspension Bridge is the Bright Angel Suspension Bridge, the silver bridge, which was built in the late 1960s to carry the cross-canyon water pipeline. Mules refuse to cross this bridge because they can see through its flooring to the river. Hikers use both bridges.

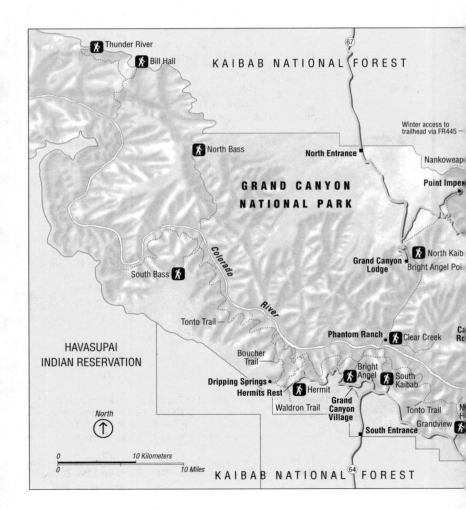

LODGING

Phantom Ranch, the only lodging facility below the c[...] on the north side of the river, more or less on a line belo[...] Canyon Village (See Park Buildings & Landmarks). Rese.vations are required for both accommodations and meals at Phantom Ranch. A backcountry hiking permit is not necessary for people staying in Phantom Ranch accommodations, but is required for any other overnight canyon hike.

The stone and log cabins have bunk beds, cold water sinks, and toilets. The nearby showerhouse is rustic in style and sparkling clean. Dormitories are separate for men and women, each with ten bunk beds, a shower and restroom. Cabins and dormitories are heated and have evaporative cooling; bedding, soap, towels, and shampoo are provided. Meals are served in the dining hall. Menus are limited and meals range in price from $6 for sack lunch to $27 for steak dinner. *Advance reservations for both lodging and meals are required*, and may be made up to one year in advance by writing or calling AMFAC Parks & Resorts ☎. *Persons with advance reservations must check in at the Bright Angel Lodge Transportation Desk one day prior to scheduled stay.* Group reservations are limited to ten males and ten females on any given day, and may be made up to two years in advance. Special restrictions apply and nonreturnable deposits are required. The Ranch is usually booked to capacity months in advance. Occasional cancellations do occur and you can check on these in person at the Bright Angel Transportation Desk in the Bright Angel Lodge between the hours of 6 A.M. and 7 P.M.

CAMPING

There are only three developed campgrounds in the inner canyon, and they are along the Corridor Trails: Indian Garden campground below the South Rim, Bright Angel campground near Phantom Ranch, and Cottonwood campground below the North Rim. All other camping permits are issued for sites with no water, toilets, emergency phones, or development of any sort.

The only permanent human habitation of the inner canyon is on the Havasupai Indian Reservation, which is at the Canyon's western end. The Havasupai Indians have occupied these ancestral lands for centuries, farming in the Canyon and raising cattle on the rim. The reservation is administered by tribal officials and is outside of park boundaries. It is accessible only by foot, horseback, or helicopter. See Attractions in the Region, Havasupai Indian Reservation.

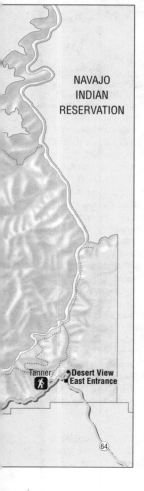

NAVAJO
INDIAN
RESERVATION

Tanner
Desert View
East Entrance

64

Colorado River

The Colorado River near Unkar Delta in eastern Grand Canyon. Photo by George H. H. Huey

The Colorado River springs from the Rocky Mountains of north-central Colorado and flows south and west 1,440 miles to the Gulf of California. Much of the river's passage is through the Colorado Plateau, a geologic province in which water, wind, and time have molded canyon-and-plateau lands that author Michael Collier calls "130,000 square miles of visual poetry." Along the way it gathers waters of the Green, Gunnison, San Juan, Paria, Little Colorado, Virgin, and Gila Rivers. Together they drain a 244,000-square-mile basin that reaches from southern Wyoming to just beyond the Mexican border and includes parts of seven western states.

The Colorado is now dammed at both ends of Grand Canyon: upriver at Glen Canyon Dam (Lake Powell), and downriver at Hoover Dam (Lake Mead). In Grand Canyon the Colorado averages three hundred feet in width and twenty-five feet in depth, and as it passes through soft, easily eroded sandstones and shales, it flows wide and smooth, often flanked by sandy beaches. When the same volume of water is constricted by narrow hard-rock gorges and fans of debris from tributaries or side canyons, rapids occur. Water velocity in rapids can be ten times greater than in the stretches of flat water in between. In 1966, boulders and rocks from a flashflood down Crystal Creek formed a debris fan that spilled two hundred feet across the river, squeezing it to one-third its previous width and creating one of its most dramatic rapids.

As the river travels 277 miles from Lees Ferry to the Grand Wash Cliffs near Lake Mead it loses almost 2,000 feet in elevation. In that distance are more than one hundred rapids, some of which drop twenty or thirty feet abruptly. All in all, they account for 90 percent of the river's elevational drop, but only 10 percent of its length.

Flowing water picks up sediment and carries it in suspension or tumbles it along the streambed. The faster the flow, the more suspension and tumbling of particles. When water flow slows, sediment particles—formally ordered by size as silts and clays, sand, gravels and cobbles, and boulders—drop out of suspension. The river accumulates sediment from its tributaries, particularly during spring snowmelt and summer thunderstorms, and before 1963 when the gates of Glen Canyon Dam were closed, by the time the river reached Grand Canyon it was red—*colorado*—and heavy with the canyon-and-plateau land's iron-oxide-saturated sediment.

Transporting silt and sand was the river's daily custom. Measurements of suspended sediment loads at Phantom Ranch from 1941 through 1957 revealed that the river moved, on the average, 85,900,000 *tons* of sand and silt through the Canyon in a year. The river carried eroded material to the Gulf of California until Hoover Dam was completed in 1936, then it carried it to Lake Mead. For twenty-five years, before Glen Canyon Dam was closed, Lake Mead had the Colorado's sediment load all to itself, and 275 vertical feet of sand and silt accumulated where river and lake meet. Since 1963, the material has settled out in Glen Canyon Dam's Lake Powell, above Grand Canyon.

The Colorado brings to these arid lands water gathered from higher, wetter places. When spring warmth melts snowpack in the river's drainage system (roughly one-twelfth of the area of the United States), the runoff enters the Colorado. Before Glen Canyon Dam checked the river, spring flows through the Canyon would swell enormously. Driftwood lines testify to a nineteenth-century flood that reached 300,000 cubic feet per second (cfs). The sediment load in such hydrologic chaos was tremendous, and the speed at which the water moved provided the needed transporting capacity. The river's water level would rise dozens of feet, obliterating plants in the flood zone and stripping away and then restoring beaches during the course of the season. When the snowmelt floods passed, the river would return to its 20,000-cfs summer average, surging again when regional midsummer thunderstorms triggered flashfloods in side canyons and tributaries.

The stated major function of Glen Canyon Dam is the storage of water, 24,300,000 acre feet of it at full pool. When this stored water is released through the Glen Canyon Powerplant's eight turbine generators it can produce 1,356,000 kilowatts of electricity. Should there be need to release more water than can pass through the turbines (33,200 cfs), it can be discharged through river outlet works. If yet more release is needed, both spillways can be opened to carry an additional 208,000 cfs between them. Of the three release methods, the turbines and their resulting power revenues are preferred.

The dam was managed to release 8,230,000 acre feet of water annually, or an average flow release of 11,400 cfs every day of the year. However, because power requirements are not constant, releases, timed to produce power when it is needed, could vary on an hourly

THE COLORADO RIVER

basis. Initially, the broad differential of release flows—which studies show often ranged from 3,000 to more than 25,000 cfs in a twenty-four-hour period—caused a "sloshing" effect on the river which stripped sand from beaches and sent waves of havoc through wildlife and plant communities. To mitigate the damage, in 1991 the United States Department of the Interior mandated that flows stay between 5,000 and 20,000 cfs and that daily fluctuations be held between 5,000 and 8,000 cfs pending further study. In 1992 President George Bush signed the Grand Canyon Protection Act which requires that the operation of Glen Canyon Dam be carried out so that it enhances the natural environment of Grand Canyon National Park and Glen Canyon National Recreation Area.

Water releases come from deep within the reservoir and are clear and very cold—forty-three degrees Fahrenheit. In June and July, the sun may warm the water to sixty degrees by the time it reaches Diamond Creek, 240 miles downstream. Pre-dam river temperatures ranged from near freezing in the winter to around eighty degrees in warm months. Native warm-turbid-water aquatic species cannot adapt to the unvarying cold. Of the eight native fish, five species have been wiped out in the Canyon, two are listed as endangered, and one is a candidate for the endangered list. Non-native fish now thrive, most notably trout.

The elimination of seasonal flooding and its beach scouring and sediment renewal has allowed erosion to the point many beaches have disappeared altogether. Sources of sediment are the river's side canyons and tributaries below the dam, and the riverbed itself. The yearly sediment load is about 11,000,000 tons (13 percent of what it once was), 70 percent of which comes from the Paria and Little Colorado Rivers. The sediment-carrying capacity of the lower flows, however, is proportionately less.

Sediment, the Department of the Interior tells us, is "literally the foundation of the riparian environment" along the river in Grand Canyon. Before the dam, floodflows scoured vegetation below the 100,000 to 125,000 cfs level, the old high water zone. The new high water zone, thirty feet lower, has added about 1,300 acres of riparian habitat within the Canyon, and plant and animal species have responded accordingly with native and non-native plants, more birds, more mammals, more insects. This new zone is, in fact, some of the most important wildlife habitat in the region. This change seems to be positive. On another happy note, trout spawning runs have begun to attract eagles, which now stop over in the Canyon to feed rather than fly through as they once did.

Dozens of studies carried out from 1982 through 1995 showed that dam operations were damaging the downstream environment, and in 1996 U.S. Interior Secretary Bruce Babbitt ordered permanent changes in dam operations. The most dramatic step, taken on March 26, 1996, was to release "flood level" flows from the dam in an attempt to duplicate the positive effects of natural floods. The seven-day flooding released flows at 45,000 cfs. Though a mere shadow of historic natural floodflows, it still brought dramatic results: rapids were partially cleared of debris, the height of many sandbars was increased about 53 percent (with sand dredged from the river bottom and redeposited on beaches), dozens of beach campsites were created, backwater habitat for native fish was increased 20 percent, and apparently no damage was done.

SILTING IN THE LAKE

When the Colorado River encounters Lake Powell's upper end, its flow slows markedly, and its suspended sediment load drops out. As one would envision, the great quantities of sediment settle out to displace many acre feet of water—868,000 acre feet in the first twenty-three years, according to a 1986 survey. Silt will fill the lake in about seven hundred years, but will reach the penstocks in three hundred to five hundred years. In the meantime, average revenues over the last ten years have been about $60.5 million annually.

Laws governing the river clash. The Colorado River Compact mandates that a certain amount of water be delivered downstream. The Endangered Species Act protects bird and fish species in the riparian zone. Federally protected American Indian cultural sites in natural flood zones become exposed and deteriorate as beaches disappear from lack of flood-replinished sand and silt. Interest groups are in conflict about water releases, and it appears that further on-purpose flooding will occur only in years when the reservoir is near full.

■ THE NORTH RIM—GETTING THERE

Today the same isolating factors that delayed tourism on the North Rim make it the less visited of the two major rim developments. The experience here is generally slow paced and quiet. You should book reservations as far in advance as possible as the North Rim is open only from mid-May until late October for overnight stays. The park is open for day use through November, or until heavy snows close the road, and visitors during that time may be required to depart on short notice. After overnight use ends there are no food, fuel, or lodging services available in the park. Travelers should be prepared for snowy roads early or late in the season. To learn opening and closing dates, contact Grand Canyon National Park ☎.

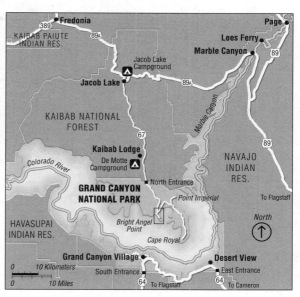

BY CAR

From Interstate Highway 15, along which lie Las Vegas, Nevada, and Salt Lake City, Utah, state highways go east to Fredonia, Jacob Lake, then south into the park, a total distance of 150 miles. The highway runs through classic canyon-and-plateau lands. The Hurricane Cliffs run north-south, and the east-west aligned Vermilion Cliffs can be seen north of the highway. West of Fredonia are the Kaibab Paiute Indian Reservation and Pipe Spring National Monument. Limited facilities and services are available along the way.

Roads go around, not across, the Canyon. Those connecting the **South Rim to the North Rim** are U.S. Highways 64, 89, and 89A, and the driving distance is 220 miles. Much of the drive is on the Navajo Indian Reservation. As the highway descends from the South Rim east to Cameron the vegetation changes from pinyon-juniper woodland to blackbrush. The Little Colorado River Overlook is about twenty miles east of the park's east entrance station. North from Cameron, Highway 89 skirts the western edge of the Painted Desert. The highway bed is on Chinle Shale, a lavender-gray rock formation that, as it absorbs

THE NORTH RIM—GETTING THERE

moisture and then dries, causes the road to heave and become rough in spots. The road runs sixty miles along the base of the Echo Cliffs. At Bitter Springs, Highway 89A continues to Navajo Bridge, which spans the Colorado River, the Canyon crossing. The Lees Ferry turnoff is just west of the river bridge. (See Lees Ferry). As the highway gains altitude it enters one of the country's largest stands of ponderosa pine. At Jacob Lake, Highway 67 runs south thirty-two miles to the boundary of the North Rim unit of Grand Canyon National Park. Food, fuel, and lodging are available at Cameron and Jacob Lake. Limited facilities and services are available in between. For the entire distance from South Rim to North Rim, the road is two lanes and heavily traveled. Many sections are hilly and curvy. During cold weather it can be icy and snowpacked. Check road conditions ☎ before you travel. Use extreme caution.

Jacob Lake, thirty-two miles north of the North Rim entrance station, provides fuel, restaurant, groceries, lodging, a privately operated RV park, and USFS campground and visitor center. Jacob Lake businesses operate year round.

Five miles north of the park entrance station are a USFS campground, Kaibab Lodge, restaurant, Country Store, and gas station.

There is only one entrance to Grand Canyon National Park's North Rim area. The North Rim Parkway runs through ponderosa forest, blending to the subalpine forest characteristic of the North Rim, stands of spruce, fir, and aspen. Numerous meadows and Crane Lake, actually a pond in a small sink-hole, are places to look for deer, elk, and perhaps wild turkeys and coyotes. (Just inside the park entrance you will find an informative meadow ecology exhibit.) Cape Royal Road turns off the parkway and travels twenty-three miles across the Walhalla Plateau to Cape Royal, with several overlook turnouts and small ancestral Pueblo occupation sites along the way. From the parkway, turnoffs for the Widforss trailhead parking lot, North Kaibab trailhead, ranger station, and campground are clearly marked. The parkway ends at the Grand Canyon Lodge parking lot. All facilities and services are on Bright Angel Point, a peninsula that juts far out into the Canyon.

Watch for wildlife

BY AIR, BUS, TRAIN, AUTOMOBILE RENTAL

The nearest major cities are Salt Lake City, Utah, 380 miles north, and Las Vegas, Nevada, 280 southwest. Both cities have regularly scheduled airline, bus, and train service, and automobile rental agencies.

BY SHUTTLE SERVICE

TRANSCANYON SHUTTLE ☎—Daily round-trip transportation between the South and North rims from mid-May through mid-October. Departs the North Rim at 7 A.M., arrives South Rim at noon; departs the South Rim at 1:30 p.m., arrives North Rim at 6:30 P.M. Reservations are necessary. Fare per person is $60 one way/$100 round-trip.

WHERE TO FIND INFORMATION

National Park Service Information Center—South end of the Bright Angel Point parking area. Park information and orientation, maps,

Grand Canyon Lodge as it appeared in 1929.

brochures, ranger-led activities, trip planning information, bookstore, restrooms, water. NOTE on hours of operation: NPS information stations and visitor centers have in the past operated on extended summer hours. This may not continue to be the case as park budgets shrink. however, you can count on their being open daily from 8 A.M. to 5 P.M.

BACKCOUNTRY OFFICE—In ranger station just north of campground. Backcountry permits, at-large camping permits, and hiking information. Open daily 8 A.M.–noon.

CONCESSIONER TRANSPORTATION DESK—Grand Canyon Lodge lobby. Commercial tours.

LODGING

For all in-park lodging reservations or information contact AMFAC Parks & Resorts ☎.

As a rule, lodging is booked well in advance. If you arrive at the park without room reservations, you may be disappointed and greatly inconvenienced. Call Grand Canyon Lodge ☎ to check on same-day reservations. If there are no cancellations available, see Lodging Outside the Park or Camping Outside the Park for other options. In-park room rates range from about $55 to $90 plus applicable taxes per night.

GRAND CANYON LODGE ☎—On Bright Angel Point. Motel units and cabins. Register at the front desk in the lodge, open twenty-four hours a day.

Union Pacific Railroad's architect, Gilbert Stanley Underwood, drew the plans for Grand Canyon Lodge and cabins as well as Yosemite's Ahwahnee Hotel, and hotels and cabins at Zion and Bryce Canyon National Parks. The lodge's enormous windows perfectly frame canyon views, and its large terraces provide ideal spots for relaxation

THE NORTH RIM

and contemplation. Registration, reception, and the dining room are in the main lodge. All guest rooms are in cabins or motel units scattered nearby in the ponderosa forest.

PHANTOM RANCH—see Inner Canyon, Lodging.

CAMPING

Camping in Grand Canyon National Park is allowed only in the campground or at-large in designated sites with a backcountry permit (See Backcountry Permits & Overnight Hiking).

NORTH RIM CAMPGROUND—NPS-operated campground. Open from late May to late October. Prices are subject to change. Water and restrooms available.

Eighty-four individual tent and RV sites (no hook-ups); $12 per site per day; maximum two vehicles and six people per site. Two accessible sites with an accessible restroom.

Four rim sites may be reserved specifically; no hook-ups; $17 per site per day; maximum two vehicles and six people per site.

Group sites for groups of 6–50 people with a sponsorship, charter, or recognition, $24.95 per site per day.

NOTE: As of late 1997 sites in this campground are available on a first-come-first-served basis. This is a temporary arrangement; park managers expect to have a reservation system in place within a few months. To check on the availability of camping reservations at the time of your trip, contact the park for the current *GUIDE*, which will contain up-to-date information. Campgrounds fill early; try to arrive before 10 A.M. to have the best chance for a site.

LAUNDRY & SHOWERS—Near North Rim Campground. Coin-operated showers; accessible restroom and showers. Open 7 A.M.– 9 P.M. daily.

The rustic Grand Canyon Lodge dining room affords spectacular views of the Canyon.

DINING & FOOD SERVICE

GRAND CANYON LODGE DINING ROOM ☎—Breakfast, full menu 6:30–10 A.M., continental menu 6:30–11 A.M.; lunch 11:30 A.M.–2:30 P.M.; dinner 5–9:30 P.M. Dinner reservations are required. Moderate to expensive.

SNACK SHOP—In Grand Canyon Lodge complex. Open daily 6:30 A.M.–9 P.M. Inexpensive.

NORTH RIM SALOON & COFFEE BAR—In Grand Canyon Lodge complex. Limited food service; open daily 11 A.M.–10:30 P.M. Inexpensive.

GENERAL STORE—Across from North Rim Campground. Open daily 8 A.M.–8 P.M. (hours may vary with demand). Pizzas, snacks, and groceries. Inexpensive.

OTHER SERVICES

FUEL—Chevron Service Station on North Rim Campground access road. Open daily 7 A.M.–7 P.M. Fuel (no diesel); propane; and minor repairs. NOTE: Diesel fuel is available at the Country Store five miles north of the park entrance, and in Fredonia, Arizona, Kanab, Utah, and Page, Arizona.

HIKING & CAMPING EQUIPMENT—See Grocery and General Store listing.

GROCERY & GENERAL STORE—Across from North Rim Campground. Open daily 8 A.M.–8 P.M. (hours may vary with demand). Groceries, camping supplies, backpacking equipment.

LAUNDRY & SHOWERS—Near North Rim Campground. Coin-operated showers. Open daily 7 A.M.–9 P.M.

LOST & FOUND—Contact the NPS Information Center.

MEDICAL SERVICES ☎—Clinic staffed by Nurse Practitioner. Located in cabin #5 adjacent to the lodge complex. Services available on a walk-in basis or by appointment. Hours: Saturday, Sunday, and Monday—9 A.M.–noon, and 3–6 P.M.; Tuesday—9 A.M.–noon, and 2–5 P.M.; Wednesday and Thursday—closed; Friday—9 A.M.–noon, and 2–6 P.M.

FOR MEDICAL EMERGENCIES dial 911 from any pay phone or residence. From your cabin/motel room dial 9-911.

POST OFFICE—In Grand Canyon Lodge complex. Window service Monday through Friday 8–11 A.M., and 11:30 A.M.–4 P.M.; Saturday 8 A.M.–2 P.M. Closed Sundays and holidays.

WORSHIP SERVICES—Catholic Mass, interdenominational, LDS services. Check bulletin board in lodge for time and location of services.

■ Facilities & Services Outside the Park

WHERE TO FIND INFORMATION	Kaibab National Forest North Kaibab Ranger District ☎ Kaibab Plateau Visitor Center, Jacob Lake, ☎ open May through October
LODGING	**KAIBAB LODGE** ☎—Five miles north of park entrance station. Open May 15–October 15.
	JACOB LAKE INN ☎—Thirty-two miles north of park entrance station. Motel, gift shop, convenience market. Open year round.
CAMPING	**DeMOTTE PARK CAMPGROUND**—USFS campground. Five miles north of park entrance station. Twenty-five sites, $10 per vehicle per night. Sites available on first-come-first-served basis. Water, pit toilets, grills, picnic tables. Free evening program. Open May through October. Pets must be on leash at all times.
	JACOB LAKE CAMPGROUND—Operated for the USFS by Southwest Natural and Cultural Heritage Association (SNCHA) ☎. Thirty-two miles north of park entrance station. Sites available on first-come-first-served basis. Water and restrooms available May through October only. Two accessible sites; accessible restroom. Picnic tables, grills. Free evening program. Pets must be on leash at all times.
	Fifty sites; $10 per vehicle per night.
	Group site; $50 per night for up to fifty people; additional $1 per night for each additional person. Call SNCHA ☎ for reservations (required).
	JACOB LAKE RV PARK ☎—Thirty-two miles north of park entrance station on Highway 67. Sixty sites with hook-ups, and fifty tent sites. Water, toilets, fire rings, picnic tables. Gates close at 9 P.M. Open May through October. Call for reservations.
	DISPERSED CAMPING ON USFS LAND—The Forest Service allows camping outside of campgrounds on forest service land. As no facilities will be provided you must *bring your own water*. Regulations are as follows:

- Carry out all of your trash.
- Bury all human waste at least four to six inches deep, a minimum of one hundred feet from water and drainage bottoms.
- Camp at least 1/4 mile away from the highway or surface water.
- Camp one mile from developed campgrounds.
- Do not camp in meadows.
- Do not dump any waste from RVs—not even gray water.
- Eliminate all signs of your campsite.

For open fires:

- Select a safe place for your open fire. Build your fire on level ground away from steep slopes, rotten logs, stumps, dense dry grass and litter.
- Clear a circle to bare dirt, being sure to remove all burnable material.
- Keep your fire small and in a shallow pit or fire pan.
- Do not build a fire on a windy day.
- Do not leave fire unattended at any time. To do so violates state and federal laws.
- Put your fire out cold before you leave. Let the fire burn down, separate the embers, mix and stir the coals with dirt and water. Make certain the fire is out by feeling it with your hands. Never bury a fire to put it out. It can escape from under the dirt. Keep mixing and stirring water into the coals until the ashes are cold to the touch.

DINING & FOOD SERVICE

KAIBAB LODGE DINING ROOM ☎—Five miles north of park entrance station. Open daily for breakfast, lunch, and dinner, May 15–October 15. Reservations recommended.

JACOB LAKE INN COFFEE SHOP & DINING ROOM ☎—Thirty-two miles north of park entrance station. Coffee Shop open year round; summer hours 6:30 A.M.–8 P.M.; winter hours 7:30 A.M.–6:30 P.M. Dining Room open summers only.

GROCERIES/SUPPLIES

COUNTRY STORE & GAS STATION—Five miles north of park entrance station. Open daily 7 A.M.–7 P.M. Groceries, camping and backpacking equipment rental and sales, and curios.

FUEL

COUNTRY STORE & GAS STATION—Five miles north of park entrance station. Open daily 7 A.M.–7 P.M. Diesel fuel, gasoline, automotive supplies.

JACOB LAKE INN & GAS STATION—Thirty-two miles north of park entrance station. Gas station open daily; summer hours 6:30 A.M.–9 P.M.; winter hours 7:30 A.M.–6:30 P.M. Propane available; no diesel. Open year round.

■ GETTING AROUND IN THE PARK

ON FOOT—The Transept Trail runs along the rim on the west side of the Bright Angel Point peninsula 1^1/$_2$ miles from the lodge to the campground. The North Kaibab trailhead is another ^{1}/$_2$ mile north of the campground.

BICYCLE—In Arizona bicycles must abide by the same traffic rules as automobiles. Use extreme caution when riding in the park, and please do not obstruct traffic. Mountain bikes are permitted on paved and dirt roads unless otherwise posted. No bicycles are permitted on any rim or canyon trails. Bikes are permitted on forest service roads outside the park. Park and Kaibab National Forest topographical maps are available at the NPS Information Center. There is no bicycle rental available in the park.

AUTOMOBILE—Park roads can become crowded on holiday weekends and during the fall when aspen leaves change color (anytime from mid-September to late October).

There is no public transportation available on the Grand Canyon National Park's North Rim. Concession tour buses and private tour buses provide services throughout the North Rim developed area.

HIKER SHUTTLE—To North Kaibab trailhead available 6 A.M.– 8 P.M. daily. $5 for first person; $2 for each additional person. Purchase tickets at Grand Canyon Lodge front desk. Pick-up point is in front of lodge.

VAN TOURS—Departure times for tours to Cape Royal and Point Imperial are posted in the Grand Canyon Lodge lobby, where tickets may be purchased.

**SERVICES
FOR SPECIAL
POPULATIONS**

The *Grand Canyon National Park Accessibility Guide*, which indicates the accessibility of most public buildings and park facilities and trails, is available free upon request at the NPS Information Center or by writing Grand Canyon National Park ☎. See Addresses and Telephone Numbers for TDD listing.

Programs, facilities, and services in the park that are fully or marginally accessible to persons with physical disabilities are noted throughout the free visitor information publication, *THE GUIDE*, with the following symbol: ♿. *THE GUIDE* is available at many locations throughout the park, including all park information centers.

United States citizens who have a physical, mental, or sensory impairment may apply in person at the NPS Visitor Center for a Golden Access Passport. These lifetime permits are free. (See Entrance Fees, Permits, and Passes) and they provide entrance to any National Park Service site.

The National Park Service provides, at no charge, wheelchairs for temporary use by park visitors. Check at the NPS Information Center.

Temporary permits for designated parking may be obtained at the NPS Information Center.

TDD telephones are available in the park to lodge guests.

Restrooms at the Ranger Station just north of the campground and Grand Canyon Lodge are wheelchair accessible. Lodge dining room and patios are accessible with a lift. Contact the Grand Canyon Lodge front desk for information.

The NPS campground has one accessible restroom and two accessible campsites.

Cape Royal Nature Trail is an accessible ¹/₂-mile paved path with minimal elevation change leading to several points with canyon views.

Point Imperial overlook is accessible.

Ranger programs that are wheelchair accessible or accessible with assistance are indicated with a wheelchair symbol in the program listing in *THE GUIDE*, North Rim Edition which is available at the NPS Information Center.

■ ACTIVITIES

RANGER-LED PROGRAMS—Presented daily on a variety of subjects and at several locations. Check *THE GUIDE*, North Rim Edition or bulletin board in the NPS Information Center for current listings.

JUNIOR RANGER PROGRAM—For young people through age fourteen. Program packets are available at the NPS Information Center.

Young visitors to Grand Canyon may participate in the Junior Ranger Program.

SEASONAL ACTIVITIES

WILDFLOWERS—All summer in mountain meadows

BIRDWATCHING—Good for the entire park season

AUTUMN LEAVES—Aspen trees can change color anytime from mid-September to late October, depending on many climate factors. It is impossible to predict precisely.

WINTER USE—Overnight winter use requires a backcountry permit (See Backcountry Permits & Overnight Hiking). Users must get into the park on foot (ski, snowshoe) from Jacob Lake, thirty-two miles north of the park entrance. Snowmobiles are not allowed anywhere in the park. The campground is available in winter but *no water, no toilet facilities, and no services of any kind* are available after the park closes to general use, from late October until mid-May.

COMMERCIAL TOURS

On the North Rim, mule trips of half- and full-day duration are available. They do not go all the way to the river. Call Grand Canyon Trail Rides ☎ for reservations.

■ RIM WALKING TRAILS

BRIGHT ANGEL POINT TRAIL—Trail begins at the log shelter in the parking area by Grand Canyon Lodge or at the corner of the east patio on the Canyon side of the lodge. This self-guiding nature trail is $1/4$ mile one way. Brochures are available in the log shelter or in the lodge.

KEN PATRICK TRAIL—Begins at the east side of the North Kaibab trailhead parking lot and goes to Point Imperial through the forest and along the rim, ten miles one way. Drainages and fallen trees make the trail difficult to follow between the Old Bright Angel Route trailhead and Cape Royal Road. Water and toilet facilities at North Kaibab trailhead; chemical toilet at Point Imperial. National park ranger Ken Patrick was killed in 1973 by deer poachers in Point Reyes National Seashore. He was the first ranger ever killed in the line of duty. Forty years old at the time of his death, he had grown up at Grand Canyon where his father was manager of Phantom Ranch. Ken Patrick is buried in Grand Canyon Cemetery on the South Rim.

TRANSEPT TRAIL—Follows the rim from the lodge to the campground. $1 1/2$ miles one way.

UNCLE JIM TRAIL—Loops off the Ken Patrick Trail and winds through the rim forest to Uncle Jim Point, overlooking the North Kaibab switchbacks. Mule riders also use this trail. The length of the Ken Patrick trailhead/Uncle Jim Point loop is five miles. James T. "Uncle Jim" Owens was the first warden for the Grand Canyon Game Reserve, serving from 1906 until 1919.

WIDFORSS TRAIL—Turnoff to parking lot is off the park entrance road two miles north of Grand Canyon Lodge. The trail runs $2 1/2$ miles one way along the rim before it turns into the forest for another $2 1/2$ miles to Widforss Point, a total of 5 miles one way. The first $2 1/2$ mile segment is a self-guiding trail; brochures are available at the trailhead. No water or toilet facilities are available. The trail is named for artist Gunnar Widforss, who lived and painted at Grand Canyon in the 1930s.

CLIFF SPRINGS TRAIL—Begins across the road from the Angels Window overlook pullout, and goes $1/2$ mile one way down a forested ravine past a small Indian settlement site, and ends at the spring. The water may be contaminated. Do not drink from the spring.

CAPE ROYAL TRAIL—A little more than $1/4$ mile one way from the southeast side of the Cape Royal parking lot to Angels Window and Cape Royal overlook. Chemical toilet in parking lot.

■ Day Hikes into the Canyon

NORTH KAIBAB TRAILHEAD TO ROARING SPRINGS

Round-trip distance: 10 miles
Vertical descent: 3,000 feet
Round-trip hiking time: 6-8 hours
**Water and toilet facilities at trailhead, Supai Tunnel, two miles down
the trail, and Roaring Springs**

Trailhead is on the park entrance road two miles north of Grand
Canyon Lodge.

The North Kaibab Trail is well developed, well marked, and
well maintained. It descends steeply to Roaring Springs at
the junction of Roaring Springs and Bright Angel Canyons.
Roaring Springs is the source for all water for Grand
Canyon National Park. Water is carried by pipeline and
stored in tanks on both rims. The North and South Kaibab
Trail segments constitute the only cross-canyon trail.

Mule day trips go as far as Roaring Springs. Mules have the
right of way on Grand Canyon trails. When you encounter
them, stand quietly to the inside of the trail and follow any
instructions given by the wrangler.

(See Day Hikes into the Canyon, South Rim, for important
hiker safety information.)

**Along the North Kaibab
Trail.** Photo by George H. H. Huey

■ OVERLOOKS

POINT IMPERIAL—At the north end of Cape Royal Road provides excellent view of Marble Platform, so called because of its level, smooth appearance, nine miles distant.

ROOSEVELT POINT—Excellent views of Marble Platform, Navajo and Hopi Indian Reservations, and Painted Desert.

WALHALLA GLADES RUIN—People of the ancestral Pueblo culture occupied this summer farming site between A.D. 1050 and 1150. Probably twenty individuals at a time lived in this pueblo and returned to Unkar Delta, in the Canyon, for the winter months. More than one hundred similar sites are scattered across Walhalla Plateau. Brochures for a self-guiding tour are available in a dispenser box.

WALHALLA OVERLOOK—Unkar Delta, the debris fan in the river bend visible from the overlook, was the site of agricultural fields used by people of the ancestral Pueblo culture about 1,000 years ago. Archaeologists believe that they lived near their river delta fields year round, with some people moving to the rim to farm during the summer months. The Walhalla Glades Ruin, across the road, was a summer farming site.

Angels Window is a natural arch near Cape Royal.

ANGELS WINDOW—Use either the small pullout near the window or the Cape Royal parking area a short distance farther.

VISTA ENCANTADA and **CAPE ROYAL** afford spectacular Canyon views to the east and south, of the Navajo Reservation on the far side of the canyon, and (at Cape Royal) a glimpse of the Colorado River.

View of Wotans Throne from Cape Royal Overlook.
Photo by George H. H. Huey

■ LEES FERRY

Above, Lees Ferry in 1900; today the beaches at Lees Ferry provide a staging ground for river trips into the Grand Canyon.

In the mid-1800s Mormons fleeing persecution in Illinois settled near the Great Salt Lake in Utah and soon began to colonize southern Utah and the Arizona Strip north of Grand Canyon. In 1857, thirty years before miners began to file claims on the Canyon's south side, Mormons, desperately fearing continued persecution, murdered a party of "gentile" (non-Mormon) pioneers who aimed derogatory and threatening remarks at church members. Full blame for the crime fell upon one participant, John D. Lee, though surely others were as guilty. To help him avoid arrest, in 1869 Mormon church leaders sent Lee to settle in a remote area at the confluence of the Paria and Colorado Rivers that missionary Jacob Hamblin had earlier noted provided the only viable crossing of the Colorado for hundreds of miles. There, just upstream from the Canyon's narrow and dark Marble Canyon, Lee established a ferry which he and his family operated until he was apprehended and executed in 1877. His wife Emma sold the ferry and ranch, known as Lonely Dell, two years later and its operation continued under various owners until the Navajo Bridge spanning the river was completed in 1928.

Ranch buildings, orchards, and a small cemetery are interpreted by Glen Canyon National Recreation Area staff.

Lees Ferry lies at the park's northeastern boundary and is accessible by paved road off of U.S. Highway 89A. It is open year round. There is a campground which is available on a first-come-first-served basis.

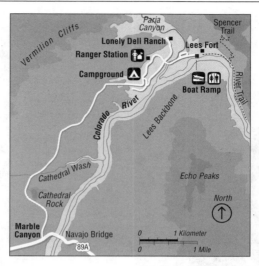

The camping fee is $10 per night. There are no hook-ups or other facilities.

This is a favored fishing spot for many. An Arizona State fishing license can be purchased at Babbitt's General Store in the South Rim Village, or at Marble Canyon Lodge near Lees Ferry.

Historic buildings at Lonely Dell Ranch.

The ferry is the put-in point for white water raft trips. It is fun to watch as boats of varying sizes and configurations are assembled and loaded with supplies, and the passengers and crew, feeling a mixture of elation and anxiety, prepare to launch into "the great unknown," as John Wesley Powell, the river's first European-American explorer, put it.

■ TUWEEP

Tuweep is in the park's remote, rugged northwestern segment. Mohave County Road 5, a few miles west of Fredonia, is the only entrance road. It is sixty miles of graded dirt and may become impassable during wet weather. Pipe Spring National Monument, on Highway 389 about twelve miles west of Fredonia, can provide information on road conditions. There is a state-operated air strip near the park boundary.

View east from Toroweap Overlook.

No water, food, lodging, fuel, transportation or any other services are available at Tuweep. The nearest town is Fredonia, sixty-nine miles away.

The elevation at Tuweep is about 5,500 feet and the landscape is made up of open spaces, grasslands, sage, and pinyon-juniper woodland. It lies on the Uinkaret Plateau in an area of obvious volcanic origin. Gently rounded cinder cones rise abruptly from the valley floor; Mt. Trumbull is to the north; Vulcans Throne, near the canyon rim, is most notable. The inner canyon configuration is strikingly different from the North and South Rim developed area views. This far west, there is no Tonto Platform to break up the vertical profile, and from Toroweap Overlook one can look right down on the Colorado River, an astonishing 3,000 feet below. Remnants of ancient lava flows that once dammed the river are still visible welded to canyon walls. Lava Falls Rapid which is one of the river's largest and most ferocious, can be seen and heard from the rim, just west of the campground.

The Tuweep Ranger Station is on National Register of Historic Places. The resident ranger uses power from on-site generators and water from the catchment system.

Area trails: Tuckup, Saddle Horse Canyon, Lava Falls Trail. Permits for overnight hiking are required. See Backcountry Permits & Overnight Hiking.

The NPS operates a free campground which is open year round. Sites are available on a first-come-first-served basis. Chemical toilets. There is *no* water. The campground may be crowded on Memorial Day and other spring and summer week-ends.

Eleven individual sites; no hook-ups; maximum eight people and two vehicles at each.

One group site; maximum eleven people and two vehicles.

■ ATTRACTIONS IN THE REGION

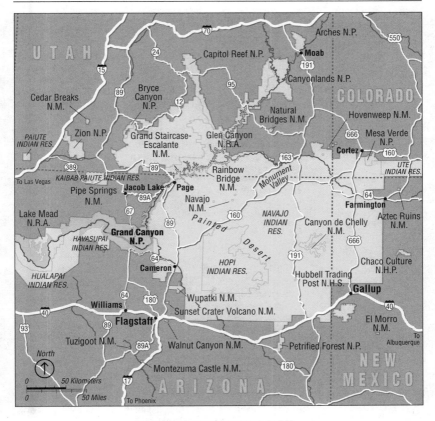

BRYCE CANYON NATIONAL PARK
Bryce Canyon, UT 84717
(435) 834-5322

Canyonlands with delicate-looking, standing red rock formations and pink cliffs. Open year round. Entrance fee. Visitor center closed Thanksgiving Day, December 25, and January 1. In-park cabins and motel rooms are available April through October. NPS-operated campgrounds open in late spring and close with freezing weather. Cross-country skiing and snowshoeing; no snowmobiling. Distance from Grand Canyon South Rim: 310 miles

CEDAR BREAKS NATIONAL MONUMENT
P.O. Box 749
Cedar City, UT 84720
(435) 586-9451

Limestone amphitheater eroded into spires, arches, and cliffs. On-site visitor center, services, and roads open June to October. NPS headquarters at Kolob Visitor Center, Zion National Park, open year round. Entrance fee. NPS-operated campgrounds open June to October. No food, lodging, or fuel available in monument. Cross-country skiing

ATTRACTIONS IN THE REGION

and snowmobiling in winter. Distance from Grand Canyon South Rim: 275 miles

CHACO CULTURE NATIONAL HISTORICAL PARK
Star Route 4, Box 6500
Bloomfield, NM 87413
(505) 786-7014

Once the center of ancestral Pueblo culture; remains of magnificent structures, including the 600-room Pueblo Bonito. Open year round. Entrance fee. Visitor center open daily. Dirt roads may be difficult in bad weather. NPS-operated campground. No food, lodging, public telephones, or services in the park. Distance from Grand Canyon South Rim: 300 miles

GLEN CANYON NATIONAL RECREATION AREA
P.O. Box 1507
Page, AZ 86040
(520) 645-2471

Glen Canyon Dam and Lake Powell, the world's most beautiful reservoir, amid sandstone slickrock and sheer canyon walls. Open year round. Entrance fee; boat-launching fee. Visitor center at dam. NPS-operated campgrounds. Concession-provided boat and equipment rentals, marinas, lodging, campgrounds, food, and other services on-site. Distance from Grand Canyon South Rim: 138 miles

HAVASUPAI INDIAN RESERVATION
Supai, AZ 86435
Tourist office, campground: (520) 448-2121
Lodging: (520) 448-2111

In western Grand Canyon, accessible by foot or horseback only. Open year round. Entry fees. Trailhead five-hour drive from Grand Canyon National Park. Eight-mile hike from trailhead to Supai Village; two more to beautiful Mooney Falls and campground. Land administered by Havasupai Indian Tribe; and lodge, campground, food, store operated by Havasupai Tourist Enterprise. Not a part of Grand Canyon National Park. Distance from Grand Canyon South Rim: 191 miles

HOPI INDIAN RESERVATION
Hopi Cultural Center
P.O. Box 67
Second Mesa, AZ 86043
(520) 734-2401

Villages on the three sacred mesas and surrounding lands are occupied by 10,000 Hopi people. Artists are known for their baskets, carved Kachina figures, pottery, and silver overlay. Visitors are welcome to the mesas, however, no photography is permitted. Food, lodging, supplies, fuel, and campgrounds. Distance from Grand Canyon South Rim to Second Mesa: 140 miles

HUALAPAI INDIAN RESERVATION
Peach Springs, AZ
(520) 769-2419

The Hualapai Indian Reservation adjoins much of western Grand Canyon. The people are known for their basketry. Visitors who wish to travel State Route 66 on the Hualapai Reservation must first obtain a permit from the tribal office at Peach Springs. Distance from Grand Canyon South Rim: 140 miles

KAIBAB PAIUTE INDIAN RESERVATION
Cultural Office
HC65, Box 2
Fredonia, AZ 86022
(520) 643-7214

Near Pipe Spring National Monument on the Arizona Strip north of Grand Canyon National Park. Distance from Grand Canyon South Rim: 211 miles

LAKE MEAD NATIONAL RECREATION AREA
601 Nevada Highway
Boulder City, NV 89005-2426
(702) 293-8907

Hoover Dam and Lake Mead; Davis Dam and Lake Mohave. Open year round. Visitor center closed Thanksgiving, Christmas, New Year's Day. NPS-operated campgrounds. Concessioner-operated boat and equipment rental, food, lodging, supplies, RV and camping sites. Distance from Grand Canyon South Rim: 270 miles

LOWELL OBSERVATORY
1400 W. Mars Hill Road
Flagstaff, AZ 86001
(520) 774-3358
24-hour recording with up-to-date schedules: (520) 774-2096

102-year-old observatory from which the planet Pluto was discovered. Day and nighttime hours. Entrance fee. Daily tours. Closed January 1 and 2, and April 26. Distance from Grand Canyon South Rim: 80 miles

METEOR CRATER
Administrative Offices
603 N. Beaver, Suite C
Flagstaff, AZ 86001
Office: (520) 774-8350
Crater site: (520) 289-2362
RV park: (520) 289-4002

Located thirty-five miles east of Flagstaff on Interstate 40. Privately owned and operated. Entrance fee. Site of meteor impact 49,000 years ago. Crater is 570 feet deep, 3 miles in circumference, nearly a mile across. Museum, gift shop, RV park, fuel, country store and other facilities on site. Open year round. Distance from Grand Canyon South Rim: 115 miles

ATTRACTIONS IN THE REGION

MESA VERDE NATIONAL PARK
Mesa Verde National Park, CO 81330
(970) 529-4461

Ancestral Pueblo cliff dwellings and other settlement sites. Open year round. Entrance fee. Visitor center open summer only. Gas, food, and lodging available in park summer only. Road may be closed periodically by winter storms. Distance from Grand Canyon South Rim via Monument Valley: 335 miles

MONTEZUMA CASTLE NATIONAL MONUMENT
P.O. Box 219
Camp Verde, AZ 86322
(520) 567-3322

Sinagua cliff dwellings, and spring-fed limestone sink. Open year round. Entrance fee. Visitor center open daily. No food, lodging, or other services in monument. Distance from Grand Canyon South Rim: 128 miles

MONUMENT VALLEY NAVAJO TRIBAL PARK
P.O. Box 360289
Monument Valley, UT 84536
(435) 727-3353 or 727-3287

Visitor Center open 7 A.M.–7 P.M. May-September, and 8 A.M.–5 P.M. October-April. Closed December 25 and January 1. Entrance fee into park boundary. Seventeen-mile scenic drive open 7 A.M.–7 P.M. in summer, 8 A.M.–5 P.M. the rest of the year. Guided tours available. Campground open April to mid-October. Food, lodging, and fuel available at nearby towns. Distance from Grand Canyon South Rim: 178 miles

MUSEUM OF NORTHERN ARIZONA
Route 4, Box 720
Flagstaff, AZ 86001
(520) 774-5213

Located on Highway 180 west of Flagstaff. Entrance fee. Dedicated to natural and human history, ancient and modern, of the Colorado Plateau. Excellent exhibits and gift shop. Special American Indian artists' exhibits and celebrations during the summer months. Open 9 A.M.–5 P.M. Closed Thanksgiving Day, Christmas Day, New Year's Day. Distance from Grand Canyon South Rim: 80 miles

NAVAJO NATION
Parks & Recreation
P.O. Box 9000
Window Rock, AZ 86515
(520) 871-6647

The largest Indian reservation in the United States, covering 17.5 million acres; population 210,000. Many towns throughout the reservation have complete services. Artists create turquoise and silver jewelry, sand paintings, woven rugs, and pottery.

NAVAJO NATIONAL MONUMENT
HC71, Box 3
Tonalea, AZ 86044-9704
(520) 672-2366 or 672-2367

Well-preserved ancestral Pueblo cliff dwellings. Open year round.
Visitor center closed Thanksgiving, Christmas, and New Year's Day.
NPS-operated campgrounds. No food, gas, or lodging in monument.
Distance from Grand Canyon South Rim: 145 miles

PETRIFIED FOREST NATIONAL MONUMENT
P.O. Box 217
Petrified Forest, AZ 86023
(520) 524-6228

The largest accumulation of petrified wood in the world; fossils, and
the Painted Desert. Open year round. Entrance fee. Visitor center may
be closed Christmas Day and New Year's Day. Road closed periodically due to winter weather. No camping or other facilities in park.
Distance from Grand Canyon South Rim: 189 miles

PIPE SPRING NATIONAL MONUMENT
HC 65, Box 5
Fredonia, AZ 86022
(520) 643-7105

Site of a perennial spring important to animal and human inhabitants
and travelers along the Arizona Strip, and fortress built by Mormon
settlers to protect grazing lands and water supply. Open year round.
Entrance fee. Visitor center open daily. Cafeteria on-site. No lodging
or gas in monument. Nearby campground operated by Paiute Indian
Tribe. Distance from Grand Canyon South Rim: 211 miles

SUNSET CRATER VOLCANO NATIONAL MONUMENT
2717 N. Steves Blvd., Suite 3
Flagstaff, AZ 86004
(520) 556-7042

Eruptions 1,000 years ago created this beautiful 1,000-foot-high
volcanic cinder cone and the dramatic lava landscape which surrounds
it. Open year round. Entrance fee. Visitor center open daily. USFS-
operated campground open summer only. No gas, food, or lodging in
monument. Distance from Grand Canyon South Rim: 75 miles

TUZIGOOT NATIONAL MONUMENT
P.O. Box 219
Camp Verde, AZ 86322
(520) 634-5564

Hilltop site of Sinagua pueblo occupied around 1,000 years ago. Open
year round. Entrance fee. Visitor center open daily. No facilities or
services in monument. Distance from Grand Canyon South Rim:
140 miles

ATTRACTIONS IN THE REGION

WALNUT CANYON NATIONAL MONUMENT
2717 N. Steves Blvd., Suite 3
Flagstaff, AZ 86004
(520) 526-3367

Beautiful small canyon filled with Sinagua cliff dwellings. Closed Thanksgiving and Christmas Day. Entrance fee. No gas, food, or lodging in monument. Distance from Grand Canyon South Rim: 80 miles

WUPATKI NATIONAL MONUMENT
2717 N. Steves Blvd., Suite 3
Flagstaff, AZ 86004
(520) 556-7040

Location of 2,000 prehistoric Sinagua occupation sites. Open year round. Visitor center open daily. No gas, food, or lodging in monument. Distance from Grand Canyon South Rim: 76 miles

ZION NATIONAL PARK
Springdale, UT 84767
(435) 772-3256

Spectacular canyons, mesas, and slot canyons. Open year round. Entrance fee. Visitor centers open daily. NPS-operated campgrounds. Lodging and food service in park. Motorhomes, buses, trailers, and other large vehicles must make advance reservations and pay a fee to be escorted through Zion Tunnel. Alternate routes are available. Distance from Grand Canyon South Rim: 272 miles

■ Canyon in a Capsule

GEOLOGY

Our Earth, a small planet orbiting a sun in an immense universe, has existed for four and one-half billion years. During that time, it hasn't had a moment's rest. Around its semi-molten interior, a cracked and uneven crust has cooled and floats in huge segments that grind against one another as they drift. The crust is upthrust into wrinkles, squeezed, stretched, churned, acted upon by nature's forces: time and gravity, time and temperature; time and wind; time and water. These movements and forces continue now and will continue as long as the earth exists. With the human perception of time, they only *seem* suspended.

Time is the Canyon's keynote. Geologic time—vast, primordial, echoing, impenetrably dark, deep time; time extending back to one-celled life and one-celled death. The oldest rock we can see at Grand Canyon, nearly two billion years old, forms the craggy walls of the Inner Gorge. It looks and feels ancient and accomplished. Gravity—the weight of overlying formations thousands of feet thick—and heat have changed it from sandstone and limestone to a dense, dark mass. For many canyon miles it is the river's bedrock, its water-and-sand-polished surface like burnished black satin along the banks. In this part of the country it forms the very basement of the North American continent, extending thousands of feet below the surface.

The craggy walls of Coconino Sandstone are actually hardened sand dunes from 270 million years ago. Photo by George H. H. Huey

In low places, things collect—windblown or waterborne sand, rock material seeking equilibrium, water in the form of oceans, lakes, ponds, and the mineral and organic matter that settles out of water. Material that would become rock layers in the canyon region was laid down by seas, swamps, and sand dunes. For millions (and millions) of years bodies of water came and went, staying in place so long that minerals and tiny animal skeletons could settle into beds hundreds of feet deep in some instances; seven hundred feet of muck from one swampy period, three hundred from another. The Coconino Sandstone amounts to a three-hundred-foot-deep layer of sand dunes, now hardened by compaction and cementation, which accumulated during a hot, dry, windswept period. Various minerals provide color to the rocks, with iron, which can be green as well as red- or orange-hued, being the most common.

When churning beneath the earth's crust slowly heaved the rock layers upward forming a huge bulge, they fractured in places and weathering and erosion began to dismantle them. The forces of erosion, simultaneous and continual through eons of layering, have been hard at work, and rock representing millions and millions of years of earth history has been stripped away. The Kaibab Limestone that today is the Canyon's rimrock was once buried in the middle of the stratigraphic stack. The overlying thousands of feet of rock, including Mesozoic-age deposits—the dinosaur record—have been worn away in this region.

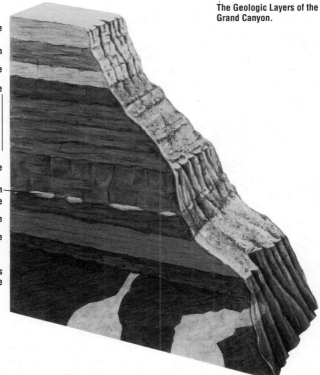

The Geologic Layers of the Grand Canyon.

Kaibab Limestone

Toroweap Formation

Coconino Sandstone

Hermit Shale

Supai Group

Redwall Limestone

Temple Butte Formation
Muav Limestone

Bright Angel Shale

Tapeats Sandstone

Precambrian Rocks
of the Inner Gorge

Deposition, plate tectonics, and erosion are ongoing global events, certainly not unique to Grand Canyon. It is the fortunate combination of natural forces that creates the scenic and scientific wonder we experience today. Six million years of fast-flowing water, most notably the Colorado River, have sculpted a canyon of truly grand countenance.

High gradient rivers tend to excavate their beds down, not out; other forces create width. Wind, water, and gravity—erosion's working partnership—relentlessly push and pull all matter downhill where, in the case of the Canyon, it lands eventually in the river. First to go would have been the river's bank, almost imaginary initially, but growing more obvious as the channel deepened. The slow action of grain-by-grain weathering of rock is the usual process, but occasional heavy runoff and, more rarely, rockfalls contribute to canyon formation. Rates of deepening and widening vary and are not steady—the process is much more "catastrophic" than we tend to imagine. Studies indicate that over the long term the Canyon probably gets about 1¹/₂ inches deeper and 15 inches wider every century on the average.

As an instrument of canyon creation, the Colorado River is ideal. Turbulent and fast-flowing, it is able to keep much gritty, abrasive

CANYON IN A CAPSULE

material in suspension as it transports it out of the Canyon and to use the same material to further grind down its channel as it goes. As the river cuts through "soft" rock layers like shale, slopes form; from hard sandstone and limestone strata, cliffs emerge, giving the Canyon its distinctive stepped profile. If the river were cutting through consistently hard rock, the canyon would be a steep V-shaped chasm. All soft rock would yield a valley rather than a canyon.

Back from the river's banks, material, once it had a place to go, began to erode from vertical fractures in the Kaibab Limestone, and variously shaped buttes were left standing within the unfolding chasm.

Equally important with the river's role as downcutting agent is its function in carrying away material that falls into its swift current. All that volume of rock that once filled the void (5,450,000,000,000 cubic yards' worth) went down the river and, until Hoover Dam was built in 1936, to the Gulf of California.

The river now lies at about 3,100 feet above sea level at Lees Ferry, dropping to 1,100 feet above sea level at Lake Mead. Downcutting will naturally slow to a crawl when the riverbed approaches sea level. The seven-to-eight-thousand-foot elevation of the land in this part of the country provides the opportunity for a very deep canyon.

Although the Canyon was not formed by a massive earthquake or volcanic eruption, both types of activity have helped shape it. Bright Angel Canyon, the north-south ranging canyon through which run the Bright Angel and North Kaibab Trails, traces an ancient fault along which significant movement and erosion have occurred over millions of years. Numerous small quakes have occurred in the region during this century. Their force has been moderate, with only a few as great as five on the Richter scale.

Silt-laden waters of the Colorado River provide one of the major erosional forces in the continuing creation of Grand Canyon.

The plateau southeast of the Canyon is punctuated with cinder cones. North of the river in western Grand Canyon, Mt. Trumbull and Vulcan's Throne are prominent eruptive volcanic landmarks. In this region, at least 150 lava flows from various sources either poured over the canyon rim or were extruded within the Canyon itself, with the result that the river was dammed a dozen or more times.

The earliest and largest lava dam, named Prospect by researchers, occurred more than a million years ago at the western end of the Canyon. Here lava flows filled the river gorge and formed a two-thousand-foot-high dam, several miles long, behind which river waters formed a lake. Prospect Lake required about twenty-two years to fill, reached to the foot of the Redwall cliffs in today's Grand Canyon Village area, and backed upstream as far as Lake Powell. When lake waters overtopped the dam they did so as a two-thousand-foot cascade, crashing into an immense plunge pool. Since the lava flow, hardened into jointed basalt columns, rested directly on river channel sand and gravel, the plunge pool quickly undercut the dam, and successive columns fell away. This, combined with the silt- and sand-laden river scouring away at the top, wore away the dam edge rather quickly, in a geologic timeframe, and the dam was destroyed in about twenty thousand years. The outrush of water carried away built-up sediment and today all that remains of this or any of the other lava dams are occasional traces of basalt clinging to canyon walls.

If geologists fantasize, and surely they do, their favorite object must be Grand Canyon. Almost everywhere else their preferred subject is wrapped in and buried under layers of itself, covered with vegetation, and usually warped. But here they can browse through a mile-deep gallery which cleanly displays layer upon horizontal layer of rock. At Grand Canyon scientists can see great expanses of rock strata, how they were laid down, in what environment, in what order, and what they are made of; they can touch them, tap upon them with rock hammers, examine their contact with other formations. Here geologic theory meets geologic reality as in no other place on earth.

CANYON IN A CAPSULE

THE PEOPLE

The record of the Canyon's human habitation took a giant leap back in time with the recent discovery of a broken and discarded spear point which archaeologists determined to be about 10,000 years old. The Paleo-Indian who made it traveled light, as did his successors, and following this spear point's shadowy message, the record of human habitation is silent for six thousand years, though surely people were here.

At least four thousand years ago hunters entered all but inaccessible Redwall Limestone caves, and in their dim recesses left small animal effigies, propitiations for good hunting. Made of willow twigs, split, bent, and ingeniously wrapped, they are readily recognized as deer and mountain sheep. Like their Paleo-Indian predecessors, these people of the Archaic Culture were hunter-gatherers. Resources were too sparse in the Grand Canyon region to allow settling down, and Archaic people kept on the move in search of food.

Ancestral Pueblo is the archaeological term for the next period, which began about 1,300 years ago. These are the people traditionally referred to as the Anasazi throughout the Southwest. Evidence shows that people of this period lived on both rims and in the Canyon, moving seasonally. They farmed throughout their canyon territory, on Colorado River deltas, and on the rims, but continued to supplement their food supply with wild plant foods and when crops were poor relied entirely on gathering. The people of this culture became the most numerous and wide-ranging of Grand Canyon's prehistoric inhabitants.

After five hundred years of occupation, ancestral Pueblo people began to leave the Canyon and were completely gone by eight hundred years ago. Though no hard-and-fast explanations can be given, there were probably several influences. Fields may have become worn out, and the growing population may have stripped wild plant and animal resources. There was a one-hundred-year drying trend which, in an already stressed environment, certainly could have made life difficult. Evidence does not bear out conflict among regional groups, so having been driven out by warfare is not likely. At any rate, the exodus was complete and widespread, involving not only the Canyon's north and south rim populations but included people from a region covering several hundred miles, most of the four-corners area.

The people probably moved to more dependable water sources, the mesas now occupied by the Hopi people and eastward to the Rio Grande Valley of New Mexico. Modern Pueblo Indians are most likely the descendants of the ancestral Pueblo. Their oral tradition teaches that settlement in the Canyon was but a point in their greater migration; they never came to stay.

The Puebloans of today live on reservations in eastern Arizona and New Mexico. The Hopi and Zuni people of today have maintained continuous spiritual ties to the Canyon, their place of emergence and the place to which the spirits of the dead return.

The Cohonina, culturally separate from the Pueblo, occupied the South Rim south to Williams and west for a four- or five-hundred-year period concurrent with the ancestral Pueblo. There is limited evidence of their occupation on the North Rim. Their lifeway was similar and their ranges seem to overlap to an extent. The Cohonina left the region at the same time as the ancestral Pueblo, but they left no trace of their subsequent movement.

About A.D. 1300, two hundred years after the ancestral Pueblo left the Canyon, two different cultural groups arrived. From the west came the Cerbat to occupy locations south of the Colorado River. In their eastward migration, part of the group, the Hualapai, chose a spot to settle; the Havasupai continued farther east to establish ancestral homelands. Along with hunting and gathering wild plants for food, they planted corn, beans, squash, sunflower, gourds, and cotton in the inner canyon. (They were still farming at Indian Garden when the park was established in 1919.) During spring, winter, and fall, they hunted game and foraged on the south rim.

The second cultural group to arrive at Grand Canyon in the 1300s were the Southern Paiute, who migrated from the Great Basin to settle on the North Rim. They may have arrived earlier. Their material culture is limited and hard to define. Hunter gatherers who farmed on a marginal basis, they followed a "seasonal round" of foraging that allowed for planting.

Athabascan ancestors of the Navajo people migrated to the Southwest from western Canada at least six hundred years ago. Their mobile lifeway, based on raiding, eventually gave way to farming as they settled near Puebloan groups and adopted their customs and skills. By the mid-1800s, Navajo people were foraging, farming, and raising livestock in and around the Canyon. Many more fled to the Canyon for refuge from round-up and incarceration by the United States military in the 1860s, and again the 1930s as the federal government forced the slaughter of animals in stock reduction programs.

EUROPEAN CONTACT

Francisco Vásquez de Coronado, with an expedition of 220 mounted soldiers, 110 foot soldiers and 1,000 Indian servants, ventured north from Mexico in 1540 on a quest for rumored abundant riches.

A contingent of the expedition visited the Hopi mesas and were told of a great river to the west. As a water route to the Pacific coast would be of great benefit to the Spanish, Coronado sent Garcia Lopez de Cárdenas and some soldiers to find it. The Hopi people furnished guides for the journey to the Canyon's south rim somewhere near the area known today as Desert View, five thousand feet above the river. After three days of searching along the rim for a route to the river, Cárdenas decided the river wouldn't be a good way to get to California, and headed back east to join Coronado. No Spaniards or others intruded upon these canyonlands for another 236 years. In 1776 Spanish priests, still searching for overland routes to connect Spanish holdings in New Mexico with those in California, passed along both north and south rims, but it was not until the mid-1800s that European-American presence became continuous and intrusive upon the land and its native cultures.

CANYON IN A CAPSULE

EUROPEAN-AMERICANS ARRIVE

Nineteenth-century Americans seeking self sufficiency on their own parcels of fertile and free land traveled trails that parted and flowed around the treacherous, inhospitable, and largely unexplored Colorado River canyon and plateau lands. Among those drawn westward in the nineteenth century were great numbers of men cut loose after the Civil War. Their hopes ran along veins of mineral ore. As they washed and backwashed around in the Southwest, they happened upon Grand Canyon, which with its surrounding lands, was in the public domain, unprotected, there for the taking. On the South Rim, mineral prospectors became the Canyon's first European-American residents, and they filed hundred of claims in the late 1800s. Though ore of various kinds—copper, asbestos, lead, silver, gold—was located, the practicalities of removing it from the Canyon and hauling it hundreds of miles to processing mills punched holes in hopes for great wealth, a decent living, or even making enough to survive. Most of the miners, given the lifeview that got them to this region in the first place, simply looked for the next opportunity, which turned out to be tourism.

From the late 1800s until 1901, their enterprises struggled along in the general area and twenty miles either side of today's Grand Canyon Village area. Visitors of the most hardy variety jolted in stages and wagons over forty or fifty miles of rocky and rutted roads. They stayed in tents and other rustic rimside accommodations, rode horses or walked down treacherous trails, along the way rubbing shoulders with honest-to-gosh miners, apparently loving every moment. Their diaries often praised the guides and the food, and always the scenery.

The fortunes of these small operators turned for the worse when the Atchison, Topeka and Santa Fe Railway bought a section of railroad from a bankrupt mining operation, completed it to the South Rim and brought in the first passenger train in 1901. Sadly for the outlying prospector/tourist operators, visitors preferred a three- or four-hour ride from Williams in a comfortable railroad car to a torturous eleven-hour wagon trip. In 1905 the luxurious El Tovar opened, with meals and service in the inimitable Fred Harvey Company style, closely followed by other facilities and services in the Grand Canyon Village area. Though the small entrepreneurs didn't give up easily, the railroad meant the end of the line for them within a few years. (Within twenty-five years after passenger rail service to the rim was initiated, most Canyon visitors arrived by automobile. The Santa Fe dropped passenger service to the Canyon in 1968.)

North of the Colorado River, things were happening differently. Mormon church leader Brigham Young and his followers left Illinois in 1844 fleeing persecution, traveled west across the plains, over the Rockies, and determined that their place was in the land of the Great Salt Lake. Young's vision was of a religious state, and he sent Mormon families out to colonize the territory. By 1851 they had founded Cedar City, and Kanab in 1864, among scores of others, and settled the Arizona Strip, that portion of land between the Canyon's North Rim and Utah's southern border. The area was, and remains today, thinly populated.

Ultimately, close park service/railroad cooperation provided much of the infrastructure for park development. The Santa Fe Railway built not only El Tovar Hotel, Bright Angel Lodge, Hopi House, Lookout Studio, Hermits Rest, the Watchtower, and Phantom Ranch, but put in the roads, built employee housing, and developed utilities. On the North Rim the Union Pacific Railway, at the urging of the park service's first director, Stephen Mather, constructed a branch from its Los Angeles/Salt Lake City main line to Cedar City, Utah. From there it provided bus tours to Zion, Bryce Canyon, Cedar Breaks, and the North Rim of Grand Canyon. It completed the exquisite Grand Canyon Lodge in 1928 and in the same year completed the water pumping station and pipelines that are still in use today.

EXPLORATION

In 1857, the United States government commissioned Army Lieutenant Joseph C. Ives to take a fifty-foot sternwheel steamboat from the Gulf of California upstream in search of a river route to get supplies to the Great Basin. After two months' striving to make 350 miles, somewhere near today's Boulder Dam the boat ran upon a submerged rock. Crew were catapulted overboard, the vessel was ruined, and Ives declared they had reached "the head of navigation." Ives and his men set out on foot and became lost in the canyon lands. Eventually, they made their way to Ft. Defiance in New Mexico Territory. Ives, in his reports, on one hand says that they gazed in delight upon the Canyon, then compares it to the gate of hell. In his judgement, "The region is, of course, altogether valueless . . . and after entering it there is nothing to do but leave." The expedition illustrator, F. W. Egloffstein, drew some dramatically gloomy images of the Canyon, not surprising after what they had been through.

John Wesley Powell, teacher, amateur naturalist, and Civil War veteran from Illinois, set out in 1869 to explore the geography and geology of the Colorado River from Green River, Wyoming, to its mouth at the Gulf of California. The Smithsonian Institution and a few other organizations supplied monetary support and scientific instruments, and the government provided military rations. Powell designed four boats, wooden and especially sturdy, in which he and a crew of nine launched from Green River, Wyoming, on May 24, 1869. By the time they reached the Paria River on August 4, they had lost one boat, many of their supplies, and did not realize the worst was yet to come—the Colossus of the river's many canyons.

Its sheer cliffs of Grand Canyon's inner gorge trapped them in a "granite prison," the immense river and its relentless rapids slammed them against rocks and walls. The men became increasingly disheartened and exhausted. Three weeks after they entered "the great unknown" at the Paria, three of the crew left the trip. They would rather take their chances finding a way up the canyon wall and then overland than spend another day on the river. These were the only men to lose their lives on the expedition; they were killed, probably by Paiute Indians still inflamed by the Indian-Mormon war of 1865–1870, on plateau lands north of the river. Had they endured a few more days with the expedition, they would have emerged with Powell at a Mormon settlement near the confluence of the Virgin and Colorado Rivers.

CANYON IN A CAPSULE

THE LANDSCAPE

Plateau lands—spare and elegant, cut by crevices and ravines, insinuations of the vast abyss that is their destination—lead to the canyon rim. They bristle with silvery-green sagebrush and stiffly waving grasses, and become seas of yellow bloom in summer. Rains leave them pungently fragrant, drooping under the weight of moisture and shining with droplets. Nearing the canyon rims, desertscrub blends into pinyon-juniper woodlands, then to stands of ponderosa pine, and on the North Rim, thick Boreal forests of spruce, fir, and aspen. The Canyon remains unannounced until one practically sets foot on the rim of its striated and chiseled expanse, a landscape of light and shadow wrapped in a brilliant, knife-edge-blue sky.

Communities and habitats blend from one to the other. Species can grow outside their usual range under "fortunate" conditions. Below the South Rim Douglas-fir, normally found only in the higher Boreal Zone of the North Rim, grows in microhabitats created in shaded crevices where, protected from drying sun and wind, moisture from melting snow or rainfall may linger.

Climate controls plant and animal life, and topography influences climate; generally, higher elevation means wetter and cooler weather. The lay of the land produces a mosaic of biotic communities or life zones: a landscape that falls or rises gently creates broad elevational belts with plant and animal communities adapted to each; steep terrain, more confined ones. Mountain peaks provide one of the most visible examples of "life zone" demarcations—timberline, an elevation above which shrubs and trees cannot grow. Nearing this limit, trees become ever more stunted and finally give way to alpine tundra. Timberline becomes higher with progression into southern latitudes: 3,500 feet in central Alaska; 12,000 feet in southern Colorado. Elevation is not the sole influence. A seemingly limitless combination of factors, topography, soil type and depth, slope aspect, growing season, and moisture among them, also come into play.

Approaching the Canyon from any direction, for fifty or sixty miles the changing plantscape records rising elevation, from sagebrush and blackbrush desertscrub at 4,000 feet to pinyon-juniper woodland to ponderosa pine, which will not grow below 7,000 feet, on to spruce, fir, and aspen above 8,000 feet. The Canyon's drop from plateau to river, greater than a vertical mile with no change in latitude, does the opposite, creating ever hotter, drier environs on the way down. On a summer day the North Rim temperature might reach 70 degrees Fahrenheit while the inner canyon temperature could top out at 115 degrees. By the time they reach the river, descending hikers will have walked from Canada to Mexico, in effect.

The plateau-and-canyon region is arid in general. The twenty-five inches of precipitation received at the highest elevations on the North Rim doesn't seem very wet unless one compares it to the inner canyon's nine.

Plants in dry climates, whether cold or hot, must efficiently use available moisture. They adapt in shape, size, growth rate, and life cycle. Typical shrub survivors have great quantities of small leaves and short stems on closely held branches, giving the appearance of being clinched against the elements, which indeed they are. Plant growth is slow in dry climates, and mature specimens often appear stunted and gnarled. Pinyon and juniper trees with trunks six or eight inches in diameter may be hundreds of years old. Pine needles, and leaves of many species of shrubs as well, are covered with a cuticle of waxy material, sealing in moisture. In some species, leaves are covered with tiny gray "hairs," which deflect sunlight and retain moisture. There are plants that, during dry times, curl their leaves to hold in every bit of moisture, unfurling them when conditions are favorable. In arid lands, many plants produce small, even tiny, blossoms. Shallow root systems spread widely, close to the surface to take advantage of even the slightest precipitation. Roots reach between and into rock crevices, anchoring against buffeting winds and scouring runoff. Many flowering plants, the annuals, sprout, bloom, and set seed when conditions are ideal, then die, leaving the seeds to begin the cycle in the next suitable season. Some go dormant during dry periods, dropping their leaves and hibernating until better times come.

Animals can migrate, hibernate, or endure seasonal changes. Many canyon mammals and birds simply travel between the rims and inner canyon as it suits them. The hot regions are occupied by many creatures that are busy during cooler nighttime temperatures and hole up during the heat of the day.

Throughout any of these zones, riparian habitats may be found along streams or seeps, regardless of elevation. Riparian plants include cottonwood, willow, horsetail, cardinal flower, monkeyflower. The riparian zone along the Colorado River includes tamarisk (non-native) and coyote willow.

Boreal Zone, North Rim plateau only—9,100 to 8,000 feet above sea level. Spruce, fir, aspen, ponderosa, mountain grasslands.

Transition Zone, both rims and plateaus—8,000 to 7,000 feet. Ponderosa pine, Gambel oak, aspen, white fir.

Upper Sonoran Zone—7,500 to 4,000 feet. Subdivided into five categories:

Pinyon-juniper woodland, both rims and plateaus, extending into inner canyon—7,500 to 4,000 feet. Pinyon pine, Utah juniper, Gambel oak, shrub live oak.

Mountain scrub, near rims and upper reaches of inner canyon—7,500 to 4,000 feet. Manzanita, silk-tassel bush, New Mexico locust, shrub live oak, serviceberry.

Desert grassland, both rims, Toroweap, inner canyon—5,200 to 3,000 feet. Blue grama, Indian ricegrass, mutton grass, squirreltail, needle and thread grass.

Sagebrush, both rims and plateaus—7,000 to 4,000 feet. Big sage-brush often interspersed with grasslands and pinyon-juniper woodlands.

Blackbrush scrub, inner canyon—5,500 to 3,000 feet. Blackbrush, yucca, Utah agave, catclaw acacia, Mormon tea, brittlebush.

Lower Sonoran Zone, Inner Gorge and western canyon regions—4,000 to 1,200 feet. Catclaw acacia, honey mesquite, creosotebush, ocotillo, brittlebush, barrel cactus.

■ ADDRESSES & TELEPHONE NUMBERS ☎

AMFAC Parks & Resorts
14001 E. Iliff Avenue, Suite 600
Aurora, CO 80014
Advance room reservations:
(303) 297-2757
(303) 297-3175 FAX

AMTRAK
Reservations: (800) 872-7245
*Information on Flagstaff
arrival/departure times:*
(520) 774-8679

Arizona Office of Tourism
1100 West Washington
Phoenix, AZ 85007
(800) 842-8257
(602) 248-1480

Bright Angel Hair Design
(520) 638-2210

Budget Car Rental
Grand Canyon Airport
Grand Canyon, AZ 86023
(520) 638-9360
(520) 779-3248 FAX

Cameron Trading Post & Motel
P.O. Box 339
Cameron, AZ 85200
(520) 679-2231

Camper Village
P.O. Box 490
Grand Canyon, AZ 86023
(520) 638-2887

CHAMBERS OF COMMERCE
Flagstaff
101 W. Santa Fe
Flagstaff, AZ 86001
(520) 774-4505
www.flagstaff.az.us

Fredonia
Box 217
Fredonia, AZ 86022
(520) 643-7241

Grand Canyon
P.O. Box 3007
Grand Canyon, AZ 86023
(520) 638-2901

Jacob Lake
(See Fredonia listing)

Williams
200 West Railroad Avenue
Williams, AZ 86046
(520) 635-4061

**Clerk of the Superior Court,
Flagstaff**
(520) 779-6535

Fredonia, Justice Court
(520) 643-7472

Grand Canyon Association
P.O. Box 399
Grand Canyon, AZ 86023
(520) 638-2481
(520) 638-2484 FAX
www.thecanyon.com/gca

Grand Canyon Day's Inn
(520) 635-9203

Grand Canyon Field Institute
P.O. Box 399
Grand Canyon, AZ 86023
(520) 638-2485
(520) 638-2484 FAX
www.thecanyon.com/fieldinstitute

Grand Canyon Lodge
(520) 638-2612
Dining room, ext. 160

Grand Canyon National Park
P.O. Box 129
Grand Canyon, AZ 86023
www.thecanyon.com/nps
General information:
(520) 638-7888
Backcountry information line
(staffed between 1 P.M. and 5 P.M.
Monday through Friday
except on federal holidays):
(520) 638-7875
*Recorded backcountry conditions
message line* (Follow recorded
instructions to reach the
backcountry information menu):
(520) 638-7888
Wedding information:
(520) 638-7761

Grand Canyon National Park Lodges
P.O. Box 699
Grand Canyon, AZ 86023
Same-day room reservations:
(520) 638-2631
El Tovar dining reservations:
(520) 638-2631
Garage: (520) 638-2631
Kennel: (520) 638-2631, ext. 6549;
for after-hours retrieval call Fire
and Safety, (520) 638-2631
Wedding arrangements:
(520) 638-2525 or 638-2565

Grand Canyon Railway
518 East Bill Williams Avenue
Williams, AZ 86046
Reservations and information:
(800) 843-8724
International calls:
(520) 773-1976
(520) 773-1610 FAX
Group sales: (800) 843-8723

Grand Canyon Squire Inn
(800) 622-6966
(520) 638-2681

Grand Canyon Trail Rides
(520) 638-2292 (summer)

**Gray Line of Flagstaff
Nava-Hopi Tours**
P.O. Box 339
Flagstaff, AZ 86001
(800) 892-8687
(520) 774-5003
(520) 774-7715 FAX

Greyhound Bus Lines
(800) 231-2222

Havasupai Tourist Enterprises
Supai, AZ 86435
Tourist Office: (520) 448-2141
Lodging: (520) 448-2111

Holiday Inn Express
(520) 638-3000

Jacob Lake Inn
(520) 643-7232

Jacob Lake RV Park
*Reservations May through
October:* (520) 643-7804
November through April:
(800) 525-0924

Kaibab Lodge
(520) 638-2389

KAIBAB NATIONAL FOREST

Kaibab Plateau Visitor Center
(North Rim)
Jacob Lake, Arizona 86022
(520) 643-7298 staffed May
through October

North Kaibab Ranger District
(North Rim)
P.O. Box 248
Fredonia, AZ 86022
(520) 643-7395 staffed year round

Tusayan Ranger District
(South Rim)
P.O. Box 3088
Grand Canyon, AZ 86023
(520) 638-2443

Kane County Travel Council
(Kanab and region)
78 South 100 East
Kanab, UT 84741
(800) 733-5263

Lost and Found—South Rim
*For items lost or found in lodges,
restaurants, or lounges:*
(520) 638-2631, ext. 6503.
For all other lost or found items:
(520) 638-7798, 8 A.M.–6:30 P.M.

Medical Services—North Rim
(520) 638-2611 ext. 222

Medical Services—South Rim
Grand Canyon Clinic:
(520) 638-2551 or 638-2469
Pharmacy: (520) 638-2460
Dentist Office: (520) 638 2395

Moqui Lodge
(520) 638-2424

North Rim Ranger Station
(520) 638-7870

ADDRESSES & TELEPHONE NUMBERS

Quality Inn
(800) 221-2222
(520) 638-2673

Red Feather Lodge
(800) 538-2345
(520) 638-2414

Road Conditions
Grand Canyon: (520) 638-7888
Arizona: (520) 779-2711
California: (916) 445-7623
Colorado: (970) 245-8800
New Mexico: (800) 432-4269
Southeast Nevada: (702) 486-3116
Utah: (801) 964-6000

Seven Mile Lodge
(520) 638-2291

Southwest Natural and Cultural Heritage Association (SNCHA)
(505) 345-9168

Taxi South Rim
638-2822 or 638-2631 ext. 6563

TDD
(520) 638-7804

Transcanyon Shuttle
P.O. Box 348
Grand Canyon, AZ 86023
(520) 638-2820

WHITE WATER RAFTING COMPANIES

Aramark-Wilderness River Adventures
P.O. Box 717
Page, AZ 86040
(800) 992-8022
(520) 645-3296
(520) 645-6113 FAX

Arizona Raft Adventures, Inc.
4050 East Huntington Dr.
Flagstaff, AZ 86004
(800) 786-7238
(520) 526-8200
(520) 526-8246 FAX

Arizona River Runners, Inc.
P.O. Box 47788
Phoenix, AZ 85068-7788
(800) 477-7238
(602) 867-4866
(602) 867-2174 FAX

Canyon Explorations, Inc.
P.O. Box 310
Flagstaff, AZ 86002
(800) 654-0723
(520) 774-4559
(520) 774-4655 FAX

Canyoneers, Inc.
P.O. Box 2997
Flagstaff, AZ 86003
(800) 525-0924
(520) 526-0924
(520) 527-9398 FAX

Colorado River & Trail Expeditions, Inc.
P.O. Box 57575
Salt Lake City, UT 84157
(800) 253-7328
(801) 261-1789
(801) 268-1193 FAX

Diamond River Adventures, Inc.
P.O. Box 1316
Page, AZ 86040
(800) 343-3121
(520) 645-8866
(520) 645-9536 FAX

Expeditions, Inc.
625 N. Beaver St.
Flagstaff, AZ 86001
(520) 779-3769
(520) 774-4001 FAX

Grand Canyon Expeditions Company
P.O. Box 0
Kanab, UT 84741
(800) 544-2691
(801) 644-2691
(801) 644-2699 FAX

Hatch River Expeditions, Inc.
P.O. Box 1200
Vernal, UT 84078
(800) 433-8966
(801) 789-3813
(801) 789-4126 FAX

**WHITE WATER
RAFTING COMPANIES**
(continued)

High Desert Adventures, Inc.
P.O. Box 40
St. George, UT 84771
(800) 673-1733
(801) 673-1733
(801) 673-6696 FAX

Mark Sleight Expeditions, Inc.
P.O. Box 40
St. George, UT 84771
(801) 673-1200

**Moki Mac River
Expeditions, Inc.**
P.O. Box 71242
Salt Lake City, UT 84171
(800) 284-7280
(801) 268-6667
(801) 262-0935 FAX

OARS/Grand Canyon Dories
P.O. Box 67
Angels Camp, CA 95222
(800) 346-6277
(209) 736-4677 OARS;
(209) 736-2924 Dories
(209) 736-2902 FAX

Outdoors Unlimited
6900 Townsend-Winona Road
Flagstaff, AZ 86004
(800) 637-7238
(520) 526-6185
(520) 526-6185 FAX

Tour West, Inc.
P.O. Box 333
Orem, UT 84059
(800) 453-9107
(801) 225-0755
(801) 225-7979 FAX

Western River Expeditions, Inc.
7258 Racquet Club Dr.
Salt Lake City, UT 84121
(800) 453-7450
(801) 942-6669
(801) 942-8514 FAX

Hualapai River Runners
P.O. Box 246
Peach Springs, AZ 86434
(800) 622-4409 outside Arizona
(520) 769-2210 or 769-2219
Hualapai River Runners is not an
NPS concessioner and is not
regulated by the NPS.

■ INDEX

■ To Learn More

Mary Colter: Builder Upon the Red Earth. Grattan. GCNHA.

The Kolb Brothers of Grand Canyon. Suran. GCNHA.

River Runners of the Grand Canyon. Lavender. GCNHA.

River Song: A Natural History of the Colorado River in Grand Canyon
  nar. by Richard Chamberlain. GCNHA Video, 40 min.

Grand Canyon National Park: A Natural History Guide. Schmidt.
  Houghton Mifflin.

A Field Guide to the Grand Canyon. Whitney. Mountaineers.

An Introduction to Grand Canyon Ecology. Houk. GCA.

Living at the Edge: A Pioneer History of Grand Canyon. Anderson. GCA.

Quest for the Pillar of Gold: The Mines and Miners of the Grand Canyon.
  Billingsley, Spamer, and Menkes. GCA.

Grand Canyon Wildflowers. Phillips. GCNHA.

An Introduction to Grand Canyon Geology. Collier. GCNHA.

A Guide to Grand Canyon Geology Along Bright Angel Trail. Thayer.
  GCNHA.

Geologic Map (Eastern Part of GCNP). Breed, Huntoon, and Billingsley.
  GCNHA.

Official Guide to Hiking the Grand Canyon (1996 revised edition).
  Thybony. GCA.

Canyon Song: A Journey from Rim to River nar. by Katherine Ross. GCA
  Video, 33 min.

(All items may be purchased from GCA by phone, FAX, mail order,
online at www.thecanyon.com/gca, or in the park sales outlets.)

■ Facts About Grand Canyon

Area: 1.2 million acres; 1,904 square miles
Length: 277 river miles Lees Ferry to Grand Wash Cliffs
Minimum aerial width: 400 feet at Navajo Bridge a few miles
 from Lees Ferry
Average rim to rim aerial width: 10 miles
Maximum rim to rim aerial width: 18 miles
Depth: 1 mile average
Rim elevations (in feet):

South Rim—	El Tovar: 6,920
	Mather Point: 7,120
	Grandview Point: 7,400
	Desert View: 7,500
	Bright Angel trailhead: 6,850
	South Kaibab trailhead: 7,200
North Rim—	Grand Canyon Lodge: 8,200
	Point Imperial: 8,800
	Cape Royal: 7,865
	North Kaibab trailhead: 8,240
Tuweep—	Toroweap Overlook/Campground: 4,450
	Tuckup Point: 6,000
	Mt. Emma: 7,700
Inner Canyon—	Indian Garden: 3,800
	Phantom Ranch/Colorado River: 2,400
	Roaring Springs: 5,000

Trails: Total miles: 400
Miles of maintained trails: 30.7

COLORADO RIVER THROUGH GRAND CANYON

Length: 277 miles
Average width: 300 feet
Minimum width: 75 feet, river level, Middle Granite Gorge, river
 mile 135
Average depth: 40 feet
Greatest depth: 85 feet
Average gradient: 8 feet per mile

NUMBER OF VISITORS

(mid-1990s) 4.5 million visitors a year to South Rim; 500,000 to
North Rim

WAYS TO GET ACROSS THE CANYON

Walk: 21 miles from rim to rim by inner canyon trails. See
Backcountry Permits & Overnight Hiking.

Drive: 220 miles (five hours), crossing the river at Navajo Bridge.
The bridge is 467 feet above the river and has a span of 834 feet. See
North Rim, By Car.

WAYS TO GET INTO THE CANYON

Walk: There are sixteen developed trails. See Inner Canyon.

Boat: Numerous commercial operations offer white water rafting trips
down the Colorado. See Commercial Tours, South and North Rims.

Mule: One-day or overnight mule trips. See Commercial Tours,
South Rim.